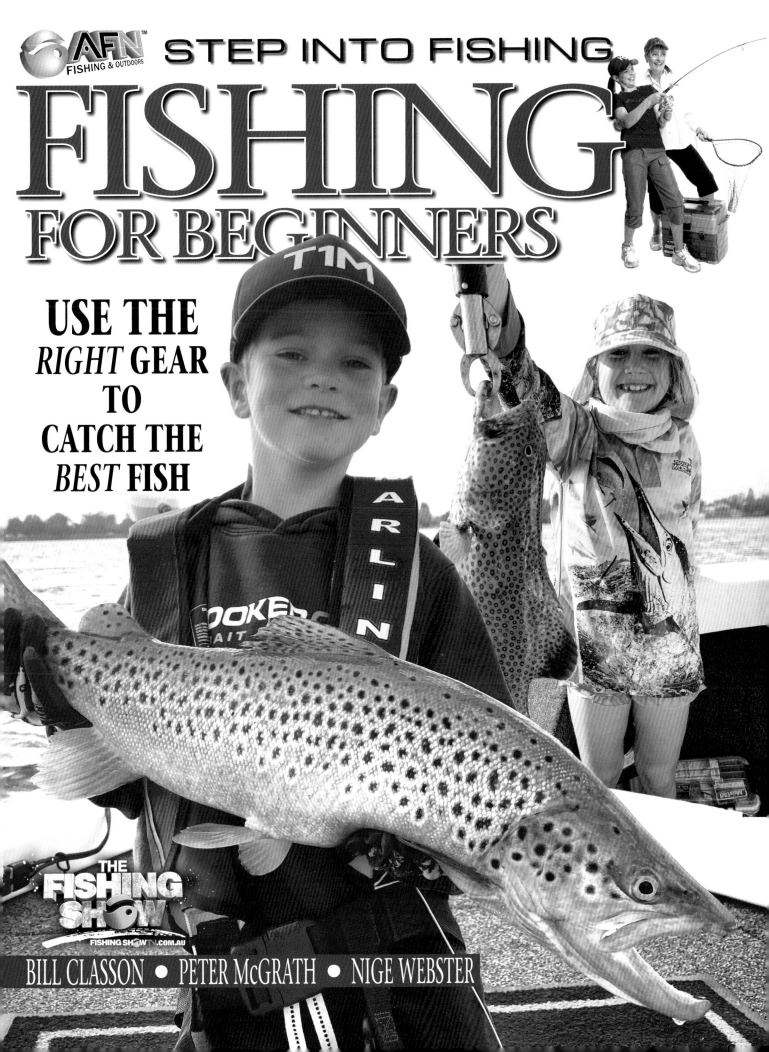

Photography: Peter McGrath and Bill Classon

First published in 2022
AFN Fishing & Outdoors
PO Box 544 Croydon, Victoria 3136
Tel: (03) 9729 8788
Fax: (03) 9729 7833
Email: sales@afn.com.au
Website: afn.com.au

Copyright © Australian Fishing Network 2022

ISBN No. 9 781865 1339 04

CONTENTS

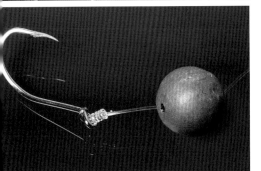

INTRODUCTION

The *Fishing For Beginners,* book is organised so that anglers of any level of experience can easily follow the steps to improve their skills.

Chapter one details the tackle that is available—and believe me, there are loads of different types of gear. We tell you what tackle is appropriate for which fish and the type of fishing and conditions in which the tackle is generally used. You will also find lots of hint boxes that will give you information on how the correct use of tackle will improve your catch. Rods, reels, hooks, lines, sinkers, floats—it's all covered.

One of the hardest things to master, yet one of the most rewarding when you get it right, is casting. In **Chapter two** we explain how to cast and how balancing your tackle will improve your casting distance and accuracy.

Learning to tie knots and rigs can be daunting, in **Chapter three** we have tying instructions for eight easy to tie knots that will cover just about everything that you need for fishing. Then we have detailed pictures and instructions for tried and proven rigs for the most commonly targeted fish.

Most anglers who take up fishing start by bait fishing. In **Chapter four** the types of bait that are used are listed and the best way of presenting them on the hook so that they are both attractive to fish and will stay on long enough to catch a fish.

An edge that most successful anglers use to attract fish from further away to their bait is berleying, and the way to mix and distribute your berley is covered in **Chapter five**.

Lure fishing is an increasingly popular method of fishing and anglers are turning to use lures sooner and sooner. **Chapter six** tells which lures are available, how best to use them and which fish they work best on.

In **Chapter seven** we reach the part that everyone wants to read. Where to fish! Here we explain what to look for in the water and along the shore that will provide the best chance of finding fish. All stretches of water are definitely not the same!

Once you have hooked a fish, you want to land it. In **Chapter eight** we explain the best ways to bring your fish in so that whether you want to keep and eat it, it is in the best condition or if you intend to release the fish, it has the best chance to survive.

While not strictly fishing, catching crabs is lots of fun and can provide a great feed. **Chapter nine** explains how to catch and handle crabs and to keep all of your fingers.

Most anglers like a feed of fish. In **Chapter ten** we detail how to clean your catch and to prepare it for cooking.

Some fish need extreme care when caught. In **Chapter eleven** we tell what precautions you should take when handling fish and list some of the fish that are particularly dangerous.

Every angler should take note of the weather forecast as the weather plays such a large part in an angler's day. **Chapter twelve** explains some of the aspects of the weather and tides that need to be considered when fishing.

All anglers need to take care of the environment and behave responsibly. In **Chapter thirteen** we look at how anglers can ensure that there are fish and places to fish for years to come.

One of the most important factors in angling is ensuring that you and the people around you are safe. **Chapter fourteen** tells of some of the dangers that fishing can expose you to and provides a list of hints to help keep you safe.

Scattered throughout the book are **fish files**—details on fish that you may catch or see, **hint boxes**—ways that you can improve your fishing or your enjoyment of the day and **fact boxes**—that provide extra information that may increase your understanding of fish, fishing or the environment.

Above all this book is intended to help anglers get started in fishing and to enjoy themselves. So get out there and start fishing—you will never stop learning.

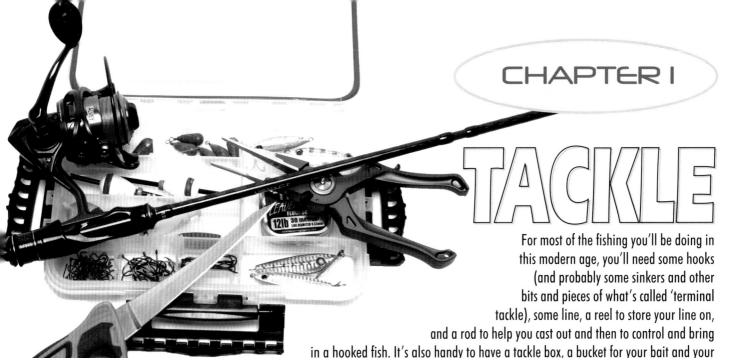

CHAPTER I

TACKLE

For most of the fishing you'll be doing in this modern age, you'll need some hooks (and probably some sinkers and other bits and pieces of what's called 'terminal tackle'), some line, a reel to store your line on, and a rod to help you cast out and then to control and bring in a hooked fish. It's also handy to have a tackle box, a bucket for your bait and your catch, and maybe a knife to trim your line, cut up bait and clean the fish you want to eat... And that's about it!

Later, as you learn more about fishing and get more involved in the sport, you might want to add bits and pieces to your collection of gear, but what I've just described will get you off to a flying start. So, let's have a look at this gear.

HANDLINES

Despite advances in fishing tackle technology the humble handline is still a great way to catch fish. Handlines are easy to carry, cost very little and catch lots of fish. They are also very sensitive and transmit every touch or bite back to the angler's index finger.

When buying handlines, just match the size of the line to the fish being sought. A light 3–4 kg handline is best for small fish up to 0.5 kg,

4–6 kg lines are good for fish up to about 1.5 kg and then you need to go heavier if you're after larger, predatory fish.

Handlines are often sold ready rigged at many tackle shops. These lines are wrapped on a cork or on a plastic spool known as a handcaster. The plastic spool can be used to store line neatly to make casting easier.

To cast with this gear, the handspool is gripped on the inside of the spool and the spool is held open faced in the desired casting direction. The other hand throws the weighted sinker using a couple of helicopter type rotations before release. With a little practice, quite good casts can be made.

The fish is hooked by holding the line between the thumb and forefinger and pulling your arm back towards your chest. Once hooked retrieve the line hand over hand

HINT BOX

How much line to put on a handcaster

All handcasters should be filled so that the line sits to at least half the depth of the spool. On deep spooled models, where such a large line capacity is not required, you can raise the line level by using a material such as string or even old line as backing. This is put on before the main line to build up the spool.

As a final point, when filling a handcaster or cork with fresh line, always remember to apply sufficient tension so that it packs down tightly and doesn't spring off the spool.

FISH FACT

THE ARCHER FISH

The archer fish found in tropical areas of Australia doesn't need fishing gear to catch its prey, it kills insects by shooting them down with pellets of water it ejects from its mouth.

Sometimes archer fish may just fire a single shot, at other times a series of shots, but whichever method is used they seldom miss. Archer fish grow to about 30 cm and 1 kg and will also take lures.

laying the line in neat coils.

If the fish is large enough to stress or break the line as it fights, ease the pressure between thumb and forefinger and let some line out. This is the most basic and sensitive drag system ever developed and good training for all anglers.

For anyone who wants to enjoy their fishing without paying too much money, a couple of handlines provide an excellent starting point.

REELS

A fishing reel is a tool for recovering and storing line. Some reels are also designed to help with casting. Others aren't. Every fishing reel has a spool of some sort to store line on, and a handle that can be turned to bring in line, as well as a foot, to allow them to be mounted to a rod. Most modern reels also have a drag or 'clutch' of some sort, that will allow line to be pulled from the reel's spool under a pre-set tension when a big fish is hooked, preventing the line from breaking.

Fact Box

TYPE OF REEL—CENTREPIN

Centrepin reels are used for luderick and fly fishing. Centrepins don't cast well and are used in very specific situations. They are effective as float fishing reels and are often the preferred reel of luderick (blackfish) anglers. You can also buy centrepin type reels that have a sidecast action to help with casting distance.

Fact Box

TYPE OF REEL—BAITRUNNER

Baitrunners are an adaption built onto threadline reels to enable fish to take a bait and move off under very light but controlled drag. This function is controlled by a lever at the back of the reel body.

These reels are designed for catching bream, snapper, mulloway, john dory, flathead and other species that need to be given line and time to swallow the bait after they take it.

The reel goes into normal fishing mode with a turn of the handle and the fish is then hooked and fought as with a threadline.

Filling the spool

When putting new line on your reel, always put the line onto the reel under finger grip type pressure and feed off the filler spool in a straight line. Do not allow the line to run off the side of the filler spool, this causes line twist.

Fill the reel to the point where the lip of the spool starts to bend outwards (*See Diagram*). A little extra line is OK but when you stop, the line should not 'jump' off the spool. If it does, you have overfilled the reel. An over full reel will be hard to manage as the line will tend to flow off the spool just as you go to cast.

Revolving drum reels also need to be correctly filled with line in order to work properly. Low line loads on revolving drum reels increases drag pressures, lowers casting distance and limits the retrieve rate of the reel.

Fact Box

TYPE OF REEL—SIDECAST

Sidecasts are a genuine, Australian product and work extremely well in any baitfishing situation. To work correctly these reels must be fished on low winch mount rods and they must carry a full line load to cast properly. Sidecast reels work best with line breaking strains from 2 to 10 kg, depending on the size of the reel. Small sidecasts are used for estuary work, particularly the 500 size. On the beaches and for shore-based fishing the 550 and 600 sizes are best.

Having no gears and virtually direct drive, these reels can handle plenty of rough work in very hard conditions. They are a good choice for beach, shore-based fishing and estuary boat angling. They come in direct drive or star drag models.

When using a sidecast, rods of medium taper provide the best casting distance. Look particularly for light rods that are easy to handle.

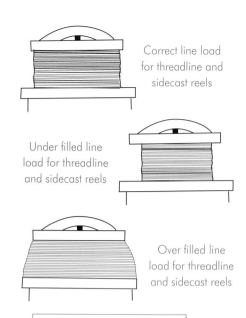

Correct line load for threadline and sidecast reels

Under filled line load for threadline and sidecast reels

Over filled line load for threadline and sidecast reels

Fact Box

TYPE OF REEL—THREADLINE

Threadlines are the most popular reel in the country. They are versatile, easy to use and very functional. They are probably the best reel for anglers just starting out in the sport because of their simplicity and ease of use.

Threadlines are also known as spinning reels or egg-beaters. They get the name from the spinning, outer rotor on the reel, which revolves around a fixed spool. The line is laid neatly onto the spool by an oscillating gear that moves the spool backwards and forwards during the retrieve.

Threadlines all have a drag system fitted to allow fish to be played under the controlled tension set by the drag. They are also geared so that for every turn of the handle, the rotor or head of the reel turns four, five or more times around the spool depending on the gear ratio.

These reels must carry a full line load to achieve good casting distance. Light lines are also needed to achieve the right balance between casting distance and fish handling ability. Most small reels work best with 2 to 4 kg lines, medium reels need 4 to 6 kg lines and large reels use 6 to 12 kg line.

The amount of line on any reel will eventually start to go down with break-offs and wear and tear. In most fishing situations it will not be necessary to refill the whole reel. Just peel back the top 100 m and add a refill to top up the spool.

Remember, don't fish with any reel that does not have the correct line load.

Fact Box

TYPE OF REEL— REVOLVING DRUM

The revolving drum reels cover everything from little baitcasters through to big game reels. Learning to cast them takes time and patience. The trick is to balance the rate at which the line leaves the spool, with the flight of the lure or bait being cast. This is done mechanically by adjusting the spool tension or cast control system and combining it with subtle control from the thumb during casting.

Good casting with these reels needs lots of practise. Once the reel is correctly adjusted and your thumb educated good casting follows naturally.

Small baitcasters are mostly used in estuaries and fresh water for lure casting and trolling. They do not cast as well into the wind as threadlines but they are very accurate at short range. These smaller reels are often fished on pistol grip type rods that provide a comfortable hand fit to the rod/reel combination.

Larger baitcasters and surf reels are fished from double handed rods to gain maximum casting power and distance. They are used from both boats and off the shore. Gear ratios are also important when analysing which of these reels to choose. High speed types of 5 or 6:1 are used for lure spinning with 4 or 5:1 being chosen for more general work.

These reels work best from medium and fast taper rods.

Caring for your drag

Drags need to be clean and free of dirt to work properly. So a clean at least once a year with white spirit is a good idea. White spirit is a cleaning solvent available at most supermarkets. Most drags are coated with a light grease to protect the washers. So make sure you re-grease the washers when you put the drag back together. If unsure how this is done, your local tackle shop can help you.

Drags also rely on having flat surfaces to run on. Always loosen the drag tension off when you put the reel away. If you put it away with a tightened drag system the washers may set or warp into that shape. This will cause the drag to be rough and jerky, causing lost fish or lost enjoyment if the equipment does not perform properly.

Setting a drag

Drag systems are provided on most reels to allow the angler to fight the fish with a preset and controlled amount of tension. The aim of the drag is to pay out line when the pull of the fish exceeds the amount of tension set on the drag. Many anglers have trouble adjusting their drag so that it both sets the hook and fights the fish correctly.

Generally, the drag should be set so that it is firm but not so tight that it will break the line. The line should slip off the reel but under controlled pressure. You can check this by tying the line to a fixed object, like a fence and then pulling with the rod and reel. The rod should curve to a firm, solid arc before the line starts slipping off the reel.

The whole purpose of the drag is to provide this slipping mechanism so the line does not break under pressure from the fish. It lets the fish run but keeps you in control.

It takes a little experimentation to get it right. If the drag ticks over in general fishing when you pull on the

rod or wind in, then it's set too lightly. If you break off when you hook the fish it is set too tightly. Always take time to set the drag correctly each time you fish. Getting the drag setting right is an essential part of catching quality fish.

did you know ...

GEAR RATIO

The gear ratio of a fishing reel is the number of times the spool rotates per turn of the handle.

For example, when one turn of the handle causes the spool to rotate three times the reel is said to have a gear ratio of 3 to 1 (sometimes expressed 3:1).

Three to one is a low gear ratio while six to one is a high ratio.

Low ratio reels are used when plenty of winding power is needed as in deep sea bottom fishing. High speed reels are mostly used when chasing fast feeding fish with lures or anywhere a fast retrieve is required to make the lure attractive to the fish.

RODS

A fishing rod is basically a stick. To be more precise, it's a flexible shaft, usually fitted with runners or guides to carry the fishing line, and a place to mount a reel.

Fishing rods offer all sorts of advantages over handlines. Rods allow you to cast further and to reach out beyond bank-side obstructions like bushes and rocks, and they keep your line off the side of a boat or away from barnacle-encrusted jetty pylons. Rods also make very useful bite indicators and shock absorbers when hooking, playing and landing fish.

However the rod must suit the type of fishing you plan to do, but with so many rods on the market it's often difficult to select which rod you need. What rods you need depends on where you fish and what you are fishing for and you may need several rod and reel combinations to get the most from your fishing.

When choosing a rod there are a few factors that you need to take into account, these are some of the important points.

Taper

A rod's taper is the rate at which the thickness of the blank narrows from its relatively thick butt to its thin tip. Most of the rods displayed in shops today are built on hollow, tubular shafts (called blanks) made of fibreglass or a mixture of graphite and fibreglass. They are light, fairly strong and fun to use, but you do need to be a bit careful with them, as they're certainly not unbreakable!

The shape of the blank

HINT BOX

One-piece rod or two?

Whether to buy a one-piece rod or two is an important decision for many anglers. What are the advantages and disadvantages?

Generally a one-piece rod has a better casting action and strength. The ferrules or sections where rods are joined, tend to slightly reduce the rod's casting action and also, marginally weaken the rod.

On the other hand, two or more piece rods are much easier to carry, particularly in cars or on public transport. For those who need the convenience of a two-piece rod, the small disadvantages are far outweighed by the ease of carriage and storage of a two-piece rod.

Modern, two-piece rods work very well and are used by most anglers at some stage. If you need a two-piece rod or just happen to like a rod that is two pieces don't worry, most will work very well.

determines the taper of the rod and the amount of fibreglass or graphite in the rod determines its weight. The accompanying illustration shows the difference in tapers and how they are classified.

Slow tapered rods are generally used in float fishing and provide a soft, uniform curve suited to handling small to medium sized fish.

Medium taper rods are very good for bait fishing. They can cast lighter weights, have a softer delivery and act as a good shock absorber when fighting strong fish.

Fast taper rods are used when casting distance is needed, particularly with lures. Fast taper rods also put more pressure or leverage on the fish during the fight.

Tip action and sensitivity is also important, it must match the type of fishing you do. Finer, lightly tipped rods tend to provide both better casting action and more 'feel' of the bites when fishing compared to heavily tipped rods.

did you know ...

TELESCOPIC ROD

A telescopic rod as the name implies, features sections that slide up inside each other for ease of storage and transport.

While telescopic rods where once seen as gimmicks, rod manufacturers today make very good models that are ideal for anyone who uses public transport or has limited carrying space. Telescopic rods will fit in a haversack, briefcase, bike carry bag or suitcase and can mean the difference between going fishing and missing out.

Maintenance is especially important with telescopic rods, and they should always be washed and wiped clean of grit and sand before being collapsed. Always store telescopic rods in their collapsed or unextended shape. This stops any chance of joints seizing or sticking together.

Rod Configuration

Surf/Rock Casting Rods
The reel can be mounted in three distinct locations on a rod. Low mounts are for sidecast reels, medium mounts are for threadlines and high mounts are for revolving drum type reels. Each mount is situated to get the most energy efficient casting position for each type of reel.

Hands

Rods used for estuary and boat casting situations are usually nominated by the number of hands used in the casting process.

Most light threadlines and baitcasters are worked on 'single handed' type rods. Only one hand is used in the casting process.

These types of rods are most commonly used for estuary and freshwater fishing.

Larger threadlines, baitcasters and

medium size revolving drum reels are worked from 'double handed' rods. Both hands are used in the casting process.

Double handed rods usually allow more power to be generated into the cast, providing greater distance with the appropriate tackle. Double handed rods are also handy when fighting tough fish for any length of time. They allow the weight of the fish to be transferred into a rod bucket rather than absorbed through the anglers wrists.

HOOKS

Don't worry too much about the different hook shapes or patterns. They all work, and you won't really need to choose specialised patterns when you're just getting started. Getting the hook's size right is far more important. As I like to say, you can catch a big fish on a small hook, but it's much harder to catch a small fish on a big hook! So, if in doubt, choose a smaller hook rather than a bigger one.

The numbering code used for hook sizing is really rather complicated. There's no easy way to explain this next bit, so pay attention while we do our best, because you'll need to come to terms with hook sizing at some stage.

Hooks range from tiny little things intended to catch tiddlers, right up to giant contraptions that look capable of holding an ocean-going ship. Their different sizes are described by a number, and this number refers to the width of the gape or gap (the distance between the point and the shank) rather than the overall length of the hook.

The really confusing part is the fact that the smallest hooks are described by the biggest numbers (I told you it was complicated!). So, a No. 24 hook isn't much bigger than the head of a pin, while a No. 12 hook is just about perfect for catching herring, small mullet and garfish, and a No. 2 is significantly larger again, and is a very good size for targeting things like black bream and redfin perch.

This sizing system, with the hook gape or width increasing as the number describing it decreases, continues until we hit No. 1. A No. 1 hook is a very useful, all-round size for many kinds of fish, from flathead, tailor and trevally in saltwater to bigger redfin and sooty grunter in the fresh. But there are a lot of larger hook sizes than a No. 1. Strangely, these bigger hooks are described by an ascending (increasing) series of numbers, followed by a slash and a

Parts of a hook

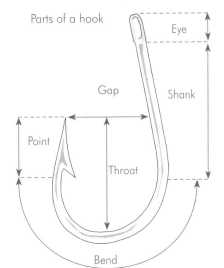

Eye

Gap

Shank

Point

Throat

Bend

Ganged Hooks
There are numerous ways to produce a ganged hook rig now. The classic method is shown at top. Other ways of linking are shown and can be purchesed across the counter at your local tackle shop.

Keeping ganged hooks
Carrying many sets of linked or ganged hooks in a tackle box can result in a tangled mess just at the time a new set is urgently needed. This can be avoided by folding up each set of hooks and wrapping it in a small square of aluminium foil. A few drops of tuna or other fish oil, smeared on the inside of the foil helps prevent corrosion.

Remember not to discard the pieces of foil carelessly where you are fishing. Either dispose of them correctly or take them home to be used again.

did you know ...

ANCIENT AND HISTORICAL FISH HOOKS

The fish hook is one of mankind's oldest tools. The original fish hooks where straight not curved like they are today. They were a length of either bone, stone, shell or deer antler that was sharpened to a very fine point at each end. The line was secured around a groove in the middle.

This 'hook' was embedded lengthwise in a piece of bait and after it was swallowed, a pull on the line would cause the pointed shaft to cross in the fish's gut.

Later, hooks started to take on the characteristic curve we associate with modern day hooks although many were still made of the same materials as the original hooks.

zero. Thus, the next size up from a No. 1 is a 1/0, then comes a 3/0, a 4/0 and so on. The very biggest hooks—intended for catching sharks, marlin and giant tuna—are in the 18/0 to 20/0 range, and would look right at home hanging from a crane on a building site!

Most of the fishing you are likely to do when you're getting started will be well covered by the hook sizes between No. 12 and about 6/0. Hooks smaller than No. 12s are mainly of interest to trout fly fishers making imitations of tiny insects, or anglers targeting very small fish to use as bait, while sizes larger than 6/0 are for people going way offshore to chase really big fish.

As the actual variation in size between each hook number is pretty small, sizes can easily be skipped when you're putting together a basic collection of hooks. So, all you really need are some No.12, 10, 8, 6, 4, 1, 2/0, 4/0 and maybe 6/0 hooks… That's plenty! In fact, if you intend fishing only in estuaries, bays, harbours or freshwater, you can skip the 4/0s and 6/0s as well.

Fact Box

Species	Size	Type
FISH SPECIES AND HOOKS		
Australian Salmon	1/0–4/0	Ganged Set (linked)/Tarpon
Barramundi	4/0–6/0	Viking/Live Bait
Bass	No.4–1/0	Suicide/Octopus
Bream	No.1–2/0	Suicide/Octopus
Flathead	2/0–4/0	Long Shank/Ganged Set
Flounder	No. 2–1/0	Baitholder
Garfish	No.10–No.6	Long Shank
Hairtail	4/0	Limerick (ganged)
John Dory	2/0–3/0	Suicide/Octopus
King George Whiting	No.6–No.2	Long Shank/Baitholder
Leatherjacket	No.10–No.6	Long Shank
Luderick	No.8	Sneck/Suicide
Mackerel	3/0–8/0	Suicide/Ganged Set
Mullet	No.8	Long Shank
Mulloway (sch)	2/0–4/0	Suicide/Octopus/Circle
Mulloway (lge)	7/0–10/0	Suicide/Live Bait
Slimy Mackerel	No.8–No.4	Long Shank
Snapper	1/0–4/0	Viking/Suicide/Octopus
Sweep	No.4–No.1	Suicide
Tailor	2/0–4/0	Ganged Set
Tarwhine	No.1–2/0	Suicide
Tommy Ruff	No.4–No.1	Viking/Long Shank
Trevally	No.4–2/0	Suicide/Baitholder
Trout	No.8–No.4	Baitholder
Whiting	No.8–No.2	Long Shank
Yellowtail	No.10–No.8	Long Shank

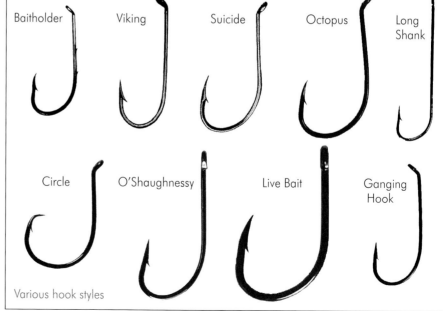

Baitholder Viking Suicide Octopus Long Shank

Circle O'Shaughnessy Live Bait Ganging Hook

Various hook styles

SINKERS

Sinkers are used to assist you to cast or to make a bait sink. They are usually made of lead and the choice of sinker weight and design depends on where you fish, the conditions being fished and the type of fish you are after. While there are many different styles and sizes, most anglers only need two or three types of sinkers and perhaps two or three different sizes of each type of sinker chosen.

In most cases, you only need enough sinker weight to make casting relatively easy but not too heavy so that it anchors the bait rigidly to the bottom.

The golden rule with sinkers is to use only just enough lead to do the job. Many fish will reject the bait because they are suspicious of the weight attached to the line.

Apart from just anchoring the bait, lead can be used to weight the line so it just sinks slowly for mid water fish. Usually small split shot are used for this.

To use sinkers properly you need to know a little bit about the main types available and how they work for you.

Types of sinkers

Ball Sinkers
The ball sinker as its name suggests, is just a ball of lead with a hole through the middle for the line. Ball sinkers cast very well and are used for shore fishing, surf casting and general fishing off jetties.

Barrel, bean and bug sinkers
These sinkers are all variations on one theme and they are used in most types of fishing. They are particularly useful in strong currents because of their reduced water resistance and low snagging qualities.

These sinkers are the best choice for drift fishing rigs and general estuary bottom fishing.

Split shot
These small ball shaped sinkers have a cut half way through them rather than a central hole. They are crimped or squeezed closed on the line using pliers. Once closed firmly they hold that position on the line.

Split shot are used to fine-tune the balance on a float and when just a tiny amount of lead is required above the bait. Jetty anglers use split shot a lot when chasing yellowtail, mullet, garfish and herring.

One thing to watch for when using split shot is not to apply too much pressure when crimping them onto the line. If too much pressure is used it can damage the line, so take care.

Snapper sinkers
These tapered sinkers with an eye at the thinner end are favoured by deep sea anglers in their larger sizes (120 g to 1 kg) and by shore casters in the smaller sizes (30 to 90 g).

The shape of the snapper sinker makes them cast straight or fall quickly to the bottom depending on their application.

Bomb sinkers
These sinkers have a 'bomb' shape with a barrel swivel moulded into the top. These sinkers are great for casting distance and for use with dropper lines and bait jigs. The swivel helps avoid line twist from either the fish or rig.

Star sinker
These are ideal for using in the surf and from jetties. They are best used over a sandy bottom as they will hold their position and resist side drift.

HINT BOX

Minimise your weight
Use as little lead as possible for most inshore fishing locations. Many fish are not bottom dwellers and they hunt for food at all levels.

A lightly weighted, natural bait will get a better reception than one anchored to the bottom. Heavy lead also tends to snag in many locations.

Bait presentation is very important in fishing and sinkers play a vital role in nearly every rig. So take care to get the sinker choice right and you will catch more fish.

FISH FACT

STARFISH—ECHINODERMS

Starfish, as their name suggests are generally shaped like a star and look slow moving and inoffensive. While some starfish are grazers others are ruthless hunters and move about quite a bit in search of their prey.

Their main prey is molluscs, shellfish of various types. They either tear them open with their powerful arms or just absorb them into their open stomach where all of their legs meet on their underside.

The starfish can actually project its stomach over its prey and eat it outside its body—sounds gruesome.

So when you see a cute, little starfish just remember, they are hunters too.

SWIVELS

Swivels are used to minimise line twist in your fishing line. They allow the fish, bait or lure to spin or twist without twisting the line.

They also serve as very convenient connectors when making fishing rigs,

Ball bearing swivel   Barrel swivel   Crane swivel   Rolling swivel

Various swivel styles

HINT BOX

Stop line twist

Line twist can be a constant problem particularly for inexperienced anglers. Fishing lines don't start with any twist its just that anglers do things that puts twist into the line. There are things you can do to avoid line twist:

- *When putting line on a reel always use a pen or screwdriver to transfer the line off the spool in a straight line. Don't wind the line off the side with the spool laying flat on the ground.*
- *Always have the drag correctly set. Every time you hear the drag click over while you are turning the handle of the reel you are putting twist into the line.*
- *The same applies when you are fighting a fish, don't just wind the reel against the fish. Lift and wind the fish. (See Fighting and Landing a Fish Chapter 8). If the drag is squawking you should not be winding.*
- *Watch if your bait spins a lot when you wind it in. Try to minimise this twisting, by keeping the bait straight.*
- *Where possible, use very small swivels to help reduce line twist.*

To remove twist from a line, the easiest way is to cut the rig off and pay out the twisted portion of the line behind a boat moving at 6 to 10 knots. All the twist will be removed from the line in a few minutes.

Land-based anglers can tie on a small ball sinker and trim the knot. Cast this out into deep water but keep the sinker off the bottom. The line twist will quickly spin out of the line.

the swivel acts as the connector for the main line and the trace and as the stopper for the sinker in many rigs.

Lure fishermen use a swivel with a snap attached to enable them to change lures quickly but very securely. However, snap swivels should not be used for bait fishing as they tend to tangle easily.

Swivels also come in a range of designs, with the brass barrel type being the most common and most popular type. Ball bearing type swivels are used in bluewater fishing to handle both the extra weight of big fish. When using swivels always choose the smallest sizes available as they work best in most fishing situations.

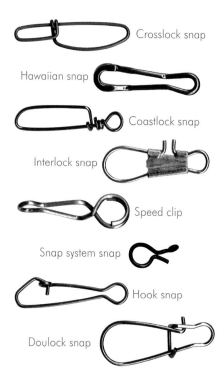

Crosslock snap

Hawaiian snap

Coastlock snap

Interlock snap

Speed clip

Snap system snap

Hook snap

Doulock snap

Various snap styles

HINT BOX

Storing terminal tackle

Terminal tackle is the term given to the equipment that you tie on to the end of your line—hooks, sinkers, swivels etc. Good quality terminal tackle is by no means cheap and, due to its size, is one of the easiest items of tackle to misplace. The best approach for storing small tackle items is to set aside a separate tackle box that fits inside your creel, basket or main tackle box.

A variety of boxes with individual compartments are available on the market. These allow for each item of terminal tackle to be stored in its own individual area.

FISH FACT

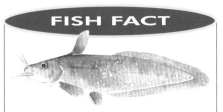

FRESHWATER CATFISH

The male freshwater catfish builds a nest in which the female lays the eggs. This nest is in the shape of a ring usually between 0.6 and 2 m in diameter. The circular component is made up of gravel and rocks with a cleared, sandy depression in the centre. The female lays up to 20,000 eggs depending on her size and the male guards these until they hatch about a week later.

TRACES

A trace is the piece of line or wire between the hook and the swivel or ring. The trace is usually a heavier piece of nylon than the main line and helps stop abrasion and break-offs from the fish's teeth, gill covers or body. Traces are also used when fishing in areas where there may be oyster covered rocks or submerged timber. On fish with sharp teeth, a wire trace may be used to prevent break-offs.

Sometimes the trace is made of lighter line to help with presentation to very shy fish. By using a trace lighter than the main line, it makes it very difficult for the fish to see and you have a better chance of the fish taking the bait. This particularly applies to fish like bream and mullet. Just remember to set the drag and fight the fish in line with the lighter trace strength.

In other fishing situations, the trace is just the same material as the main line. For example, when fishing for dart, whiting and similar table fish a special trace is not required. Just use your main line to make the rig. This is common practice.

Always remember that traces are extremely important because they are the link between you and the hooked fish. Pay attention to tying the knots

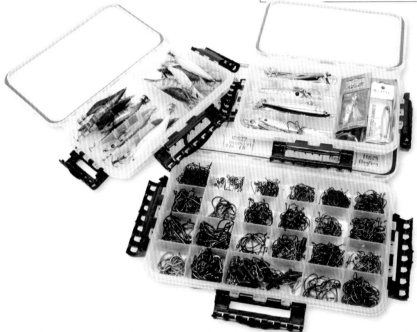

Wherever possible keep your tackle in boxes by fishing type or for specific fish and keep the tckle separated so that all of one size and type is by itself.

RINGS

Two types of rings are used in fishing, split rings and solid brass rings.

Split rings are used on lures to enable the fitting and changing of hooks. They are made of either stainless steel or nickel plated mild steel.

Solid brass rings are just a little circle of solid brass. These rings are used in rigs as a strong connector, particularly in game fishing or when using heavy lines.

Rings make great connectors. Line to line or hook to lure.

HINT BOX

Tailor and wire traces

Tailor can sever nylon line with their sharp teeth, yet surprisingly few bite-offs occur when fishing with ganged hook rigs or lures. This is largely because the fish's tail-biting attack generally results in a lip or mouth hook-up that leaves the tailor chewing on hook shanks or the lure's body.

However, very large tailor can easily engulf a smaller lure or bait, and if fish over 2 kg are anticipated, a short length of light wire is good insurance. Wire may also be needed when using live baits or fish strips on single hooks.

correctly and make sure this vital part of the rig is right. The best and most appropriate knots to tie for each part of the trace are shown in chapter 3 of this book, along with detailed tying diagrams and instructions.

did you know ...

TEETH OF A SHARK

Different kinds of sharks have different shaped teeth and this is one of the characteristics that scientist use to distinguish the individual species.
Tiger sharks have triangular shaped teeth. This allows them to feed on a broad range of prey.
The great white shark also has triangular shaped teeth that are much bigger than those of the other sharks. When the jaw closes the upper and lower teeth act like serrated scissors.
The mako shark has slender teeth that help it grasp its prey, allowing the shark to swallow its meal whole.
There are many other species of sharks in Australia and all have specific shaped teeth to help them with their particular feeding method

LINES

Fishing lines have all sorts of characteristics that need some consideration: stretch, colour, softness, diameter, price and so on. Of these breaking strain and diameter are the most important.

Breaking strain and diameter

It is not valid to talk about breaking strain without looking at the diameter

of the line as well. Different brands have different diameter lines for the same breaking strain and each has its uses. So, it is necessary to choose what will best suit the type of fishing you do.

The line size must also suit the reel being used. Putting 20 kg line on a small threadline reel will just about stop you from casting any distance, its just too heavy. The line must also sit well on the reel and cope with wear and tear and the line strength (breaking strain) must comfortably handle the average fish being sought.

You will generally catch more fish by fishing with lighter lines but it must be kept in perspective, don't fish too light or you might be broken off easily. For most estuary fishing, 3 to 4 kg breaking strain is ideal, on the beach 6 to 10 kg line is needed, while offshore anglers use 15 to 25 kg lines.

Thin lines cast better than thick lines and allow you to cast light weights with greater ease.

So when you look at fishing lines look both at the breaking strain and the diameter. The diameter will be

HINT BOX

Matching line and casting weight

When lure or bait fishing, it is important that the breaking strain of the line matches the weight of either the lure or sinker and the bait. Light sinker or lure, light line should be the rule. Use the following table as a guide.

Breaking strain	Optimum casting weight
1 kg	4 to 10 g
2 kg	10 to 14 g
3 kg	14 to 18 g
4 kg	18 to 28 g
5 kg	18 to 35 g
6 kg	28 to 42 g
7 kg	28 to 48 g
8 kg	28 to 56 g
9 kg	40 to 90 g
15 kg	60 to 120 g
24 kg	90 to 200 g

shown in millimetres. For an average 3 kg line it will be 0.25 mm, for a thin 3 kg line it will be 0.20 mm or even 0.18 mm. The only drawback here is that ultra thin lines tend to cost a lot of money. It is often better to stay with a good quality, medium thickness line than to pay huge amounts for very thin lines.

The softness of the line lets it sit snuggly on the reel while the stretch adds a type of shock absorber effect when fighting a fish. All nylon fishing lines stretch when under load.

Memory in fishing lines refers to the coils it can gain from being wound onto a spool under tension. Some lines retain these coils, which can be very annoying to anglers.

Fishing lines can be coloured for various reasons. Game fishing anglers often use bright yellow lines so the skipper can see them easily against a blue sea while fighting a fish. Anglers chasing shy fish like bream or blackfish prefer more natural colours like green, brown or blue so the line fades into the background. For most fishing choose lines with a natural or neutral colour as these usually produce the best results.

Braided lines

Braided or gelspun fishing lines are very popular in many forms of fishing. These lines have a very low diameter for breaking strain, often being half as thick or even a third as thick as a conventional nylon line of the same strength. They also have little or no stretch and so convey every bite or strike very directly to the angler.

Braided lines are used very heavily by anglers fishing deep water. This thin line has less 'drag' through the water and is less effected by current. Bite sensitivity is also increased as is the ability to hook the fish.

Lure casting and trolling anglers also use braid because of its sensitivity and instant hook up capacity. The fine diameter of the line allows the easy casting of small lures and soft plastic type jigs.

The only down side to braided lines is the cost. They are very expensive when compared to nylon line.

FLOATS

Floats serve several roles for the angler. The float as its name suggests 'floats' or suspends a bait at a

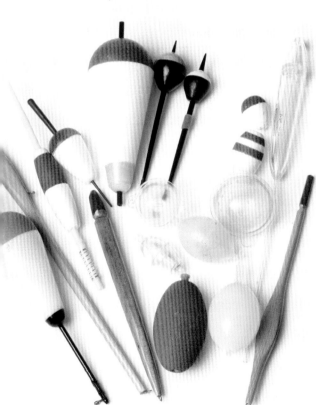

Fact Box

LATERAL LINE
The lateral line, which can be seen running along the side of a fish is actually a collection of sense receptors which can pick up minute vibrations in the water. It acts like ears and touch for the fish.

The lateral line assists fish in keeping together in schools without touching when they cannot see each other at night. During the day vision may play a large part in this, but at night, each fish will respond to the water pressure caused by another fish moving towards or beside it so that all the fish in a school will move in unison.

desired depth, the depth at which the angler believes the fish will be feeding. This depth can be easily adjusted with most floats. The float is also a bite indicator with the movement of the float telling the angler what the fish is doing to the bait.

Floats come in a very wide variety of shapes and sizes to suit all sorts of fish and fishing situations.

Most floats are made from buoyant material including foam, plastic, cork, wood and even porcupine quills.The floats also come in a range of colours to help the angler see them when fishing. Light colours are used for still, dark waters and red, orange or yellow for choppy or turbulent conditions.

Types of floats

Quill Float: Used in reasonably calm waters and usually set on the line using the plastic pressure rings that come with these floats. The line is threaded through the rings, which are then placed on the top and bottom of the float rather than running along the line. The quill float can be easily adjusted to hang baits at different depths. It is particularly popular with anglers fishing for blackfish, garfish and some freshwater species.

Pencil Float: A somewhat heavier style favoured by garfish and mullet anglers. The pencil float is virtually a large quill. It is used where there is a little chop on the water and a slight current, it is also useful for estuary blackfish.

Stemmed Float: This is the typical blackfish float, but can also be used for mullet. It has a cork or foam body with a stem of cane, dowel or aluminium. It can be rigged either fixed or running.

Bubble Float: These round or football shaped floats are often chosen by trout anglers using mudeyes, worms and other natural baits. Plugs or holes allow the float to be partially filled with water, allowing the water to be used as the casting weight.

Bobby Cork: Usually designed to slide freely up and down the line and stop at a particular depth. The bobby cork is a firm favourite with rock fishermen. It allows them to suspend baits in rocky spots that would otherwise snag a conventional rig. Bobby corks give greater distance and accuracy in casting than most other float designs.

Moulded Floats: Moulded floats usually have the weight built in and are very useful for presenting unweighted baits to shy or touchy fish. They are very good on mullet, garfish, bream and carp.

Feeder Floats: These floats or float attachments are filled with berley which then slowly enters the water around the baited hook (See Berley Chapter 5). Feeder floats are very useful for mullet, garfish, tommy ruff and carp fishing.

Rigging a float

Most floats are designed to ride upright in the water. If after casting, you find that the float is lying on its side, it either needs more lead or the lead is set too deeply and is resting on the bottom. It may also be tangled.

Some floats are moulded with the balancing weight within them. These floats in their smaller sizes are excellent for fishing with an unweighted rig beneath the float. This type of rig is very productive on mullet, garfish and other surface feeding fish.

No matter what type of float you use, it should be balanced to sit the way you want it. This balance is provided by using split shot or small sinkers to achieve the desired result. As a rule, the fish should be able to pull the float under the water with very little resistance, so the float should be weighted to sit with most of the float under the water.

The depth at which the float is suspended is set by using a 'stopper'

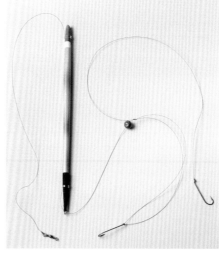

Smaller varieties of fish or baitfish are often caught on tackle that includes a centrepin reel and a pencil or quill float.

which is usually small enough and soft enough to pass easily through the rod runners. Most tackle shops sell 'float stoppers' which are designed to slide onto your line and they make the job of fitting a stopper as simple as possible. The stopper needs to be large enough to stop the float moving past the desired depth, but small enough to easy pass through the guides of the rod being used.

When to strike

Part of the fun of using a float is being able to see what is happening with your bait. Watching the float carefully, tells you exactly what is happening, all you need to do is set the hook at the right time to hook the fish.

When the float bobs up and down it means something is attacking the bait, if it goes under or moves steadily in one direction it usually means the fish has shown a definite interest and has taken the bait.

Different types of fish will take the bait in different ways. Mid water fish like mullet, garfish, yellowtail, tailor and tommy ruff usually feed fast. When fishing for these with small, soft baits and little hooks a quick strike is usually needed. Fish like blackfish, leatherjackets, bream, carp and trout are often far more cautious about the bait and need a little time to take it properly.

Big predatory fish taking a whole pilchard or live bait under a float will usually consume the bait whole and will be hooked as soon as you raise the rod to set the hook.

TACKLE BOX

Everyone needs a tackle box of some kind to store the gear they take fishing. For some anglers it is just a plastic container with some hooks, sinkers and swivels. For others, it's a multi-shelf, flip top, high tech mobile tackle shop. Most anglers just need something that keeps their essential gear neatly ordered, protects it from the elements and is easy to carry around.

The contents of the tackle box will depend on the type of fishing being done, but in general the following is fairly standard equipment needed by most anglers.

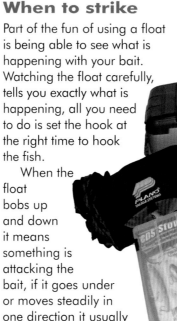

Tackle boxes are available in all shapes, sizes and materials. Select one that holds all of your tackle for a specific fish species or method of fishing.

Hooks

Hooks are best stored in a small, plastic containers within the tackle box. Little plastic boxes with clear lids are ideal. The reason for this is that the hooks can go everywhere if the tackle box falls over. Having them in a small box also helps keep them dry which prevents rusting.

Only carry enough hooks for a couple of trips, if you carry lots of hooks they'll mostly end up rusty.

Sinkers

Sinkers are heavy, too many sinkers will make your tackle box uncomfortable to carry. So, just as with hooks, only carry what you will need for a couple of trips. Keep the sinkers in the bottom of the tackle box. If you put them in the shelves they tend to unbalance the box when you open it. The smaller sinkers can be placed in the tackle compartment box with your hooks.

Swivels

These are small items, with most anglers using size 10 to size 4. Twenty or should be plenty.

Knife

Choose a knife that has a scaler on

Fact Box

STINGRAY'S TAIL

As everyone now knows stingrays can really hurt or even kill you. The barbed spine at the base of a stingrays tail is its defensive weapon against attackers or threats. The ray can arch over and drive the spine very accurately into its attacker.

The spine is large, sharp, serrated and sits in a surrounding sheath that carries a very painful poison. The wound from a stingray can also become very severely infected if not thoroughly cleaned and treated with antiseptic.

These are dangerous animals and anglers should just cut them off and let them swim away. Don't handle them or mess about with them. They are part of the marine eco-system and deserve plenty of respect.

the back, it will make cleaning the fish easier and saves carrying a separate scaler. A knife is an essential fishing tool used for cutting bait, trimming knots, cleaning fish and other odd jobs. Keep your knife clean and sharp but always take care when using it.

Sharpening stone

A small, fine grained carborundum stone is necessary to keep both your knife and hooks sharp.

Pliers

A pair of long nosed pliers is needed for crimping sinkers onto the line, trimming knots, cutting wire, tuning lures and for removing hooks from fish with teeth. This can be stored in the bottom of the tackle box.

Cutters

A pair of sharp cutters are a great working tool when making rigs and trimming line. They are a neat, cheap and safe way to work the line.

Lures

Lures are like hooks, only carry what you need and what works where you are going to fish. It is fairly pointless carrying barramundi lures around if

HINT BOX

Squid Jigs

One other possible addition to the tackle box is a squid jig. Without a doubt, the prawn imitation style jigs are very effective squid takers. Cast the lure out and allow it to sink but always watch the lure or the line as the squid will often seize it as it sinks. If this happens, wind fast and lift the rod to set the hooks.

Otherwise, just wind the lure in slowly using the rod tip to impart a gliding, twitching action to the lure. The squid can strike savagely and fight hard, but constant pressure will bring them to the net.

Once caught they can be used for bait or turned into a very tasty meal.

Squid jigs are available in a vast range of colours and sizes.

you are fishing in Port Phillip Bay. But a couple of small lead fish or chrome spoons would be handy for bay trout (salmon), barracouta, pike or tailor.

Along with your lures it is also worthwhile including a packet of bait jigs.

Ruler or measure

Always carry something to measure your fish. It is important that you do not keep undersized fish, so a ruler can be a handy guide. Some tackle stores have stick on labels in the form of a ruler. This could be stuck on the outside of your tackle box to save space.

Spare line

A spool of spare line is always handy. Anglers can often lose a bit of line through snags, tangles or even a big fish. Having a spare spool of line means you can just join the lines, top up your reel and keep fishing. The spare spool can also be used as a handline if you need it.

did you know ...

AIR BLADDER

Air bladder, gas bladder or swim bladder is a gas-filled sac located in the middle-dorsal section of a fish's body. The air bladder provides an internal float to keep the fish at a constant depth in the water without the necessity for the fish to be constantly swimming.

The amount of air in the bladder is regulated, enabling the fish to rise or descend in the water. The gas is usually a mixture of oxygen and nitrogen. Sudden changes of depth can cause the bladder to expand quickly and the stomach or bladder may be pushed out of the fish's mouth by the pressure. This can be seen when deep water fish are hauled to the surface.

Some fish lack swim bladders. In the case of saltwater bottom-dwelling species like flounder, they have no need of one. However, surface and mid water species without air bladders, including tuna, swordfish, marlin and sharks must remain constantly in motion to avoid sinking.

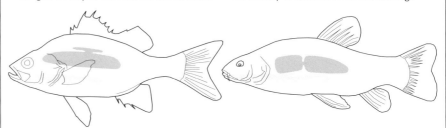

The air bladders of the tench (right) and perch (left). In species such as tench, carp, trout and freshwater salmon, there is a duct that links the air bladder to the intestinal tract, enabling the fish to absorb and release air directly through the mouth. In perch-like fish, this duct is absent and the fish relies on glands to absorb and secrete gas.

Fact Box

Pocket Guides

Many anglers carry a pocket guide or fisheries booklet with them so they know what fish they've caught or what the rules are. A small tide table is also very useful and these are normally available free from most good tackle shops.

CHAPTER 2

CASTING

Two things are important when casting: distance and accuracy. In most situations, accuracy is the more important of the two. To achieve both distance and accuracy the tackle must be right. The reel should be correctly filled with line and the rod must be appropriate for the style of fishing being done. If the tackle is right, the rest is up to you.

In all situations, even with beach and rock fishing try to cast somewhere, don't just cast anywhere.

In many forms of fishing, casting accuracy is essential to success. Lure casting for trout, bass, flathead, tailor and even tuna demands accurate work. Anglers fishing with bait also need to be very particular about where they cast and how they cast.

Good casting develops with practice, books like this and others only give the theory and some guidelines. When casting, always concentrate on what you are doing and try to get it right. If the cast goes too high the release has been made too early. If the bait or lure slams into the water close by, the release has been made too late.

Work on getting a smooth flow of energy through the rod and into the cast. Don't force it though, this only

Fact Box

KEEP IT TOPPED UP

The amount of line on the reel spool is important in all fishing to achieve both casting distance and retrieve speed.

Any reel that is low on line will not cast well. This particularly relates to threadline and sidecast reels. If you cast when the spool is low on line, the line hits the lip of the spool as it travels off. As it does so, it slows down and this causes a loss in casting distance.

Overhead reels lose distance too, this is because the spool has to spin faster at the start of the cast to achieve casting speed and to maintain the casting distance.

The amount of line on the spool also influences the retrieve. The greater the spool size, the faster the retrieve. If the spool is only 75 per cent filled, then you will lose 25 per cent of the retrieve speed.

All anglers should keep their reels full of line to ensure maximum performance from their tackle.

causes more problems. Start with short casts and work from there.

Once you achieve a comfortable casting style, both distance and accuracy will improve so long as you continue to demand the results from yourself.

Remember, all tackle has its limits and you can only achieve results within the capacity of the gear. Also, your peak accuracy will be at about 80 per cent of your maximum casting distance so keep that in mind when casting at particular targets.

Learn to use a variety of casting styles. You should be able to cast from both the right and left hand sides and from directly overhead. This is particularly important when working in crowds or from a small boat or on a tree-lined shore.

In the end, good casting should become a reflex action with the bait or lure going just where you want it. Don't be afraid to make mistakes, it all takes time and practice.

Balancing the casting weight with the tackle is also very important. It is impossible to make powerhouse casts with a beach rod loaded with 3 kg line and a 90 gram sinker, the line will just snap every time. The sinker is just too heavy for the breaking strain of the line. Change the line class to 10 kg and it will work. Drop the line class to 6 kg and the sinker weight to 60 grams and again a workable ratio is available. The whole secret is balancing the tackle.

When choosing lures for casting, weight must also be considered. In many cases some very good lures are

just too light for accurate casting.

Lures that don't cast well frustrate the fishing process. Try to choose lures that balance with the casting capacity of the tackle being used.

The right way to cast the main types of tackle are shown in the following pages.

HINT BOX

Iron out casting problems
When your reel is full of line and the rod, reel and casting weight is in balance, the rest is up to the angler. While most people learn to cast as part of a day's fishing, casting can be improved with a little specific practice.

If you have some spare time, then go to a sandy area with no snags and try a little casting practice. Change things like the amount of power you apply, sinker sizes, the way you release the line and when you release the line.

Just take the time to get it right. Casting is like any sporting skill, the more you do it the easier and more natural it gets.

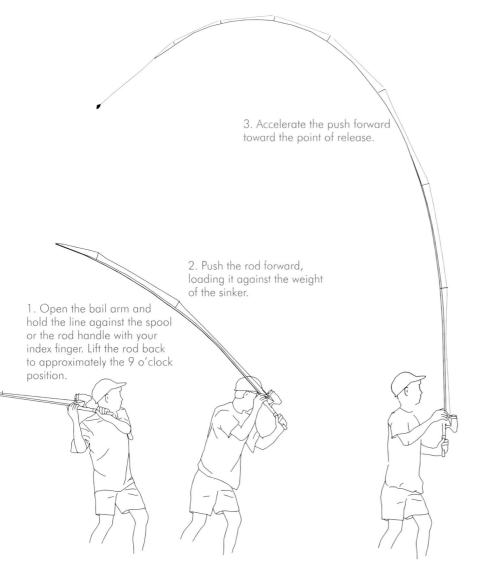

3. Accelerate the push forward toward the point of release.

1. Open the bail arm and hold the line against the spool or the rod handle with your index finger. Lift the rod back to approximately the 9 o'clock position.

2. Push the rod forward, loading it against the weight of the sinker.

Casting with a double handed threadline. Power should be applied by pushing forward with the top hand (the right hand in the case of a right handed person), and pulling back towards the body or thigh with the hand holding the rod butt.

4. As the rod approaches the vertical release the line from your index finger to allow the rig to take the line from the spool and lower the rod tip to point it in the direction of the cast.

CHAPTER 3

KNOTS & RIGS

Knowing how to tie reliable knots is an essential part of fishing and many anglers who are just starting get confused with the choice. Fortunately there are a number of knots that are quite easy to tie and work very well. In this section we will outline the various knots required and then show which one goes where when constructing a rig.

KNOTS

Whether you fish salt water, fresh water, beach, rocks, offshore or estuary, lures or bait there are only a few knots that you will need to master. For tying hooks, rings and swivels to monofilament fishing line there are two simple and effective knots that can be used—the **locked half blood knot** and the **uni knot**. Which one to use is your choice, have a try at tying each and see what is the easiest for you to master. If you intend to do some beach, rock or pier fishing you will need to master the **blood bight dropper** so you can attach sinkers to your rigs and to attach your hooks to the rig.

If you are going to try some lure fishing, and who doesn't give it a go at some stage, then a simple lure loop knot is needed and the **leftys loop** is an easy way to attach a lure to your line. The reason for the use of a loop to attach lures is that minnow lures in particular work much better with the flexibility of a loop than with a knot that closes right up on the eye of the lure. Sometimes you'll need to attach a leader to the end of your line; this is necessary if casting in the surf and sometimes when lurecasting or trolling lures for bigger fish. The easiest and best way to attach a leader is the **Albright knot**, which has the added advantage of being able to join any lines of different breaking strains.

Finally, there are a couple of knots that could be needed for particular circumstances. If you are fishing offshore and using heavy leaders for sport and game fish then a knot that works with heavy line to attach a hook is required—the **thumb knot** is a pretty easy way to go in this case. A simple way to attach your line to the reel to spool up and start fishing is the **arbor knot**. If you want to use braid or super lines, and more and more anglers are venturing there, then you will need to attach a leader of monofilament to the end of the braid so you can attach a lure or a rig. As braid is smooth and has a much finer diameter than mono of the same breaking strain, knots tied with braid can slip and let go. More turns and locks are required; a **double uni knot** is the easiest way to attach a mono leader to braid.

When tying knots, always lubricate them with some saliva before pulling them up tight. Tightening up on dry mono can cause friction to burn the line and weaken the knot.

So there are really only three or four knots that are required to get you out there effectively fishing. Work out the easiest and see how it matches up in the rigs that you intend to use in the next section.

Locked Half Blood knot

This knot is also sometimes referred to as the improved clinch knot. It is a simple and strong knot for a variety of purposes, and very easy to execute.

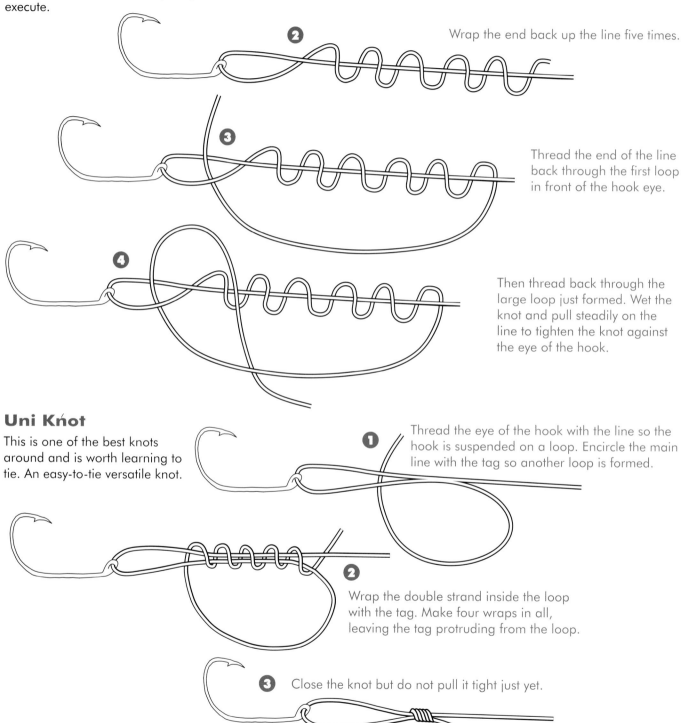

1 Thread the line through the hook eye.

2 Wrap the end back up the line five times.

3 Thread the end of the line back through the first loop in front of the hook eye.

4 Then thread back through the large loop just formed. Wet the knot and pull steadily on the line to tighten the knot against the eye of the hook.

Uni Knot

This is one of the best knots around and is worth learning to tie. An easy-to-tie versatile knot.

1 Thread the eye of the hook with the line so the hook is suspended on a loop. Encircle the main line with the tag so another loop is formed.

2 Wrap the double strand inside the loop with the tag. Make four wraps in all, leaving the tag protruding from the loop.

3 Close the knot but do not pull it tight just yet.

4 Slide the knot down onto the eye of the hook, pull it tight and trim the tag.

ENEMIES OF NYLON LINE

Nylon fishing line has a number of enemies the most important being abrasion, bad knots and sunlight.

Abrasion

Sand, rocks, barnacles, faulty rod runners and other obstacles can give lines a tough time. Care should be taken to stop line dragging over rough surfaces. You should also check that the rod runner, bail arm rollers and level wind carriers are in good condition to minimise abrasion which can cause the line to break suddenly.

Bad knots

Lines have good strength provided the knots you use are tied carefully and correctly. Always take care to tie good knots and lubricate them with salvia as they are tightened.

Sunlight

Although it happens very slowly, the ultra violet rays in sunlight have a damaging effect on fishing line. The effect of the sun from a days fishing is small but don't store reels where they will be in direct sunlight, like opposite a garage window. It will make the line last longer and help retain its working properties when out on the water.

Blood Bight Dropper Knot

This knot is used to make loops that stand off the main line, to which you can attach your hooks. Additionally you can tie a Blood Bight at the end of the rig and use it to attach your sinkers. This is a very important knot when making rigs to fish off piers, rocks, surf and jetties. It is also used when bottom fishing offshore and in bays.

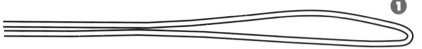

Double the line back to make a loop of the size desired.

Bring the end of the loop twice over the doubled part.

Now pass the end of the loop through the first loop formed in the doubled part.

Draw the knot up into shape, keeping the pressure on both lines.

Leftys Loop

This knot is about the easiest of the entire lure loop knots to master and is equally effective on light or heavy lines. When locked it doesn't slip and it has a very high knot strength, well over 90 per cent, so it can be used with leaders or just straight onto the main line.

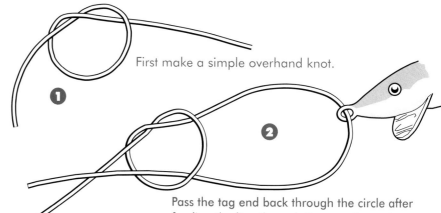

First make a simple overhand knot.

Pass the tag end back through the circle after feeding the line through the eye of your lure.

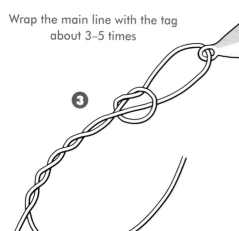

Wrap the main line with the tag about 3–5 times

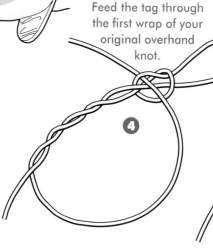

Feed the tag through the first wrap of your original overhand knot.

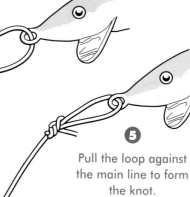

Pull the loop against the main line to form the knot.

Albright Knot

The Albright knot is a standard knot for joining lines with two different breaking strains and is ideal for joining a leader to the main line if you want to lure fish or sportfish offshore and need a heavier line to your hook or lure. This is an optional knot to learn and only needed if you require a rig in the following section that specifies this knot.

Form a loop in the tag end of the heavier line making sure that you allow about 15 cm to overlap. Take the lighter line and pass the tag through the formed loop.

Pinch both lines about 8 cm from the end, and at the same time allow 8 cm of the lighter line to protrude beyond this point to tie the knot. Start winding the lighter line back towards the end loop.

Make at least ten turns of the lighter line back over the doubled section. Pass the lighter line through the end loop on the same side of the loop that the lighter line originally entered.

Very slowly pull on the lighter line ends while grasping the heavier line and working the coils of the knot towards the loop end. Do not allow the coils to slip off the loop.

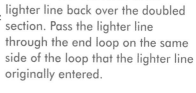

Thumb Knot

This knot is the one to use if you are using the heaviest monofilament 30–100 kg breaking strain. It may be that you are live baiting for tuna or mulloway or trolling offshore with big lures. With really heavy monofilament you need a knot that allows you to tighten and lock it. The locked half blood and uni knots are not suitable here.

This is an optional knot to learn and only needed if you require a rig in the following section that specifies this knot.

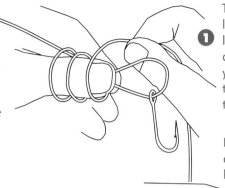

① Thread your hook with the line and make a loop so that the hook is suspended from the loop. Pinch the crossover between the thumb and finger of your left hand. Start wrapping your left thumb and loop with the tag. Make three wraps in all, woprking the base of your thumb toward the thumbnail.

② Push the tag back under those three wraps alongside your thumb. Push it all the way back toward the base of your thumb. Secure the tag against your left thumb with your middle finger.

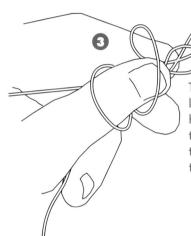

③ Then take the hook loop in your right hans and ease the wraps off your thumb, one at a time in sequence.

④ Close the knot by exerting pressure on the loop against the tag.

Double Uni Knot

Many anglers starting will soon give super lines or braid a go. When you do you will need a knot that allows you to attach a mono leader to your braid. The double uni knot is a good one to master, as it is just an extension of the uni knot. It's easy to tie and is reliable regardless of the difference in diameter of the monofilament and the braid being connected.

This is an optional knot to learn and only needed if you require a rig in the following section that specifies this knot.

① Run the lines to be joined parallel and then take one tag end and form a loop over the other line.

② Wrap the tag through the loop and around the lines four or five times.

③ Draw the knot together.

④ Repeat the process with the other tag end.

⑤ Lubricate both knots and then pull them together.

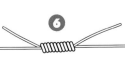

⑥ Then take the tag ends to clinch the knots tight. Pull on the lines again to ensure that the knots are snug. Trim off the tags.

Arbor Knot

This is a very fast and secure knot for attaching line to the reel.

Pass the tag end of the line around the spool and form an overhand knot with the tag end around the main line. Then another overhand knot on the tag end of the line.

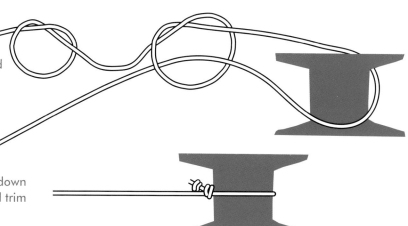

Lubricate the lnots, tighten down by pulling the main line and trim the tag.

RIGS

There are hundreds of different rigs that can be used and anglers invent, adapt and adjust rigs to suit the conditions and their needs. Rigs are the business end of your tackle and a good rig that presents the bait or lure naturally to the fish will catch fish.

The selection of rigs shown here will give any angler a great start on how to set up for a particular fish or a style of fishing. When setting up your rig remember to use sharp hooks—chemically sharpened are great if you can afford them—and make sure that all your knots are secure and well tied.

Also make sure that you've got the right style and size hook for the fish that you are targeting.

There are a number of basic styles of rig that cross over all aspects and types of fish and fishing situations. For each one there are dozens of subtle variations that can be made to suit the specific fishing situation.

Running Sinker Rig

This is one of the most basic rigs used to catch fish that feed on or near the bottom. It works best in shallow to medium depth water (1–10 metres). A running sinker rig consists of a sinker threaded onto the line with a hook at the end and in its simplest form the sinker runs all the way to the hook.

A swivel, split shot or ring can be added to separate the sinker from the hook and in this form it is one of the most widely used rigs in fishing. It is effective in fresh and salt water, rivers, estuaries, bays and lakes. It can be adapted for big species such as mulloway and is equally effective with smaller fish such as bream and whiting.

Dropper Rig or Paternoster

If you have to cast a long way, in the surf or off the rocks, or if you're fishing offshore in deep water or in a fast flowing river for native fish then a variation of this rig is perfect. The sinker in this rig always is located at the end or bottom of the rig and hence the hooks are always located up the line and off the bottom. Hence it is ideal for using on rough or reefy bottoms; it is also perfect for surf fishing as it keeps the bait off the turbulent sandy bottom.

Fixed sinker rigs

These are where the sinker is fixed to the line or have their movement up and down the line restricted to somewhere along its length, but not at the end. These rigs are ideal for smash and grab fish like tropical species—barramundi and mangrove jack.

Mid water rigs

These are very simple and essentially are just a hook on the end of the line allowing the bait to move and drift freely through the mid water. Usually the bait itself is the casting weight, but a small piece of fixed lead or split shot can aid casting and also pull the bait down to the desired depth. Often anglers will use ganged hooks in this situation.

Float Rigs

There are hundreds of different float rigs and they are very popular in fresh water as trout are mid water feeders and are always looking for suspended baits. Float rigs are designed to suspend the bait at a level where the fish are feeding. The floats used in these rigs can be anything from delicate balsa floats to large polystyrene floats or even inflated balloons for suspending big live baits for tuna.

HINT BOX

Stalking the fish

Many fish feed and are caught in shallow, often clear water. Approaching these fish and presenting a bait or lure to them demands a level of hunting skill, stalking the fish. Experienced anglers try to sneak up on the fish. They move slowly and deliberately using polaroid sunglasses to identify where the fish are holding.

When stream fishing always keep well back from the water. Keep low and look for rocks and bushes that can give you cover. Work the fishiest areas with as little disturbance as possible before moving up to the water's edge.

When wading or moving around again move slowly and positively and make sure your foothold is good or you may slip and fall.

With the boat, always slow down before reaching the fishing area and idle into the area or use an electric motor or oars for a really quiet approach.

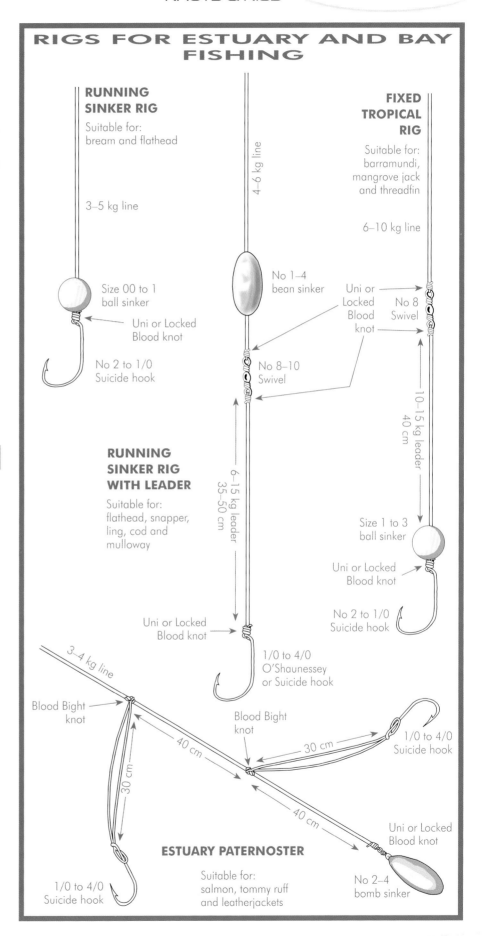

RIGS FOR ESTUARY AND BAY FISHING

RUNNING SINKER RIG
Suitable for: bream and flathead

3–5 kg line

Size 00 to 1 ball sinker

Uni or Locked Blood knot

No 2 to 1/0 Suicide hook

FIXED TROPICAL RIG
Suitable for: barramundi, mangrove jack and threadfin

6–10 kg line

4–6 kg line

No 1–4 bean sinker

Uni or Locked Blood knot

No 8 Swivel

No 8–10 Swivel

10–15 kg leader 40 cm

Size 1 to 3 ball sinker

Uni or Locked Blood knot

No 2 to 1/0 Suicide hook

RUNNING SINKER RIG WITH LEADER
Suitable for: flathead, snapper, ling, cod and mulloway

6–15 kg leader 35–50 cm

Uni or Locked Blood knot

1/0 to 4/0 O'Shaunessey or Suicide hook

3–4 kg line

Blood Bight knot

30 cm

40 cm

Blood Bight knot

30 cm

1/0 to 4/0 Suicide hook

40 cm

Uni or Locked Blood knot

ESTUARY PATERNOSTER
Suitable for: salmon, tommy ruff and leatherjackets

1/0 to 4/0 Suicide hook

No 2–4 bomb sinker

RIGS FOR ESTUARY AND BAY FISHING

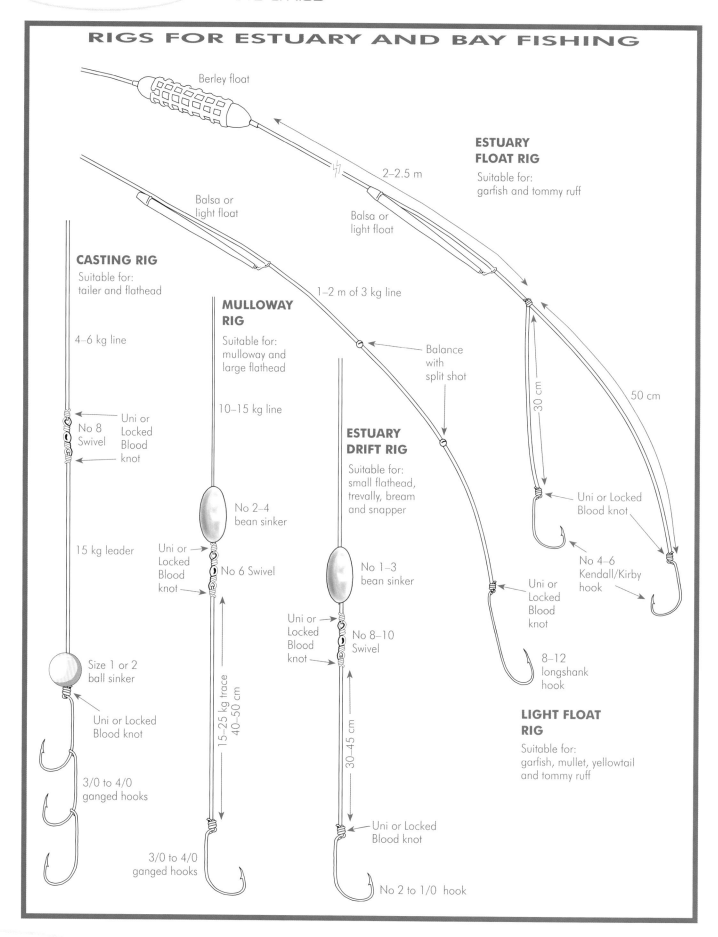

Berley float

**ESTUARY
FLOAT RIG**

Suitable for:
garfish and tommy ruff

2–2.5 m

Balsa or
light float

Balsa or
light float

CASTING RIG

Suitable for:
tailer and flathead

4–6 kg line

**MULLOWAY
RIG**

Suitable for:
mulloway and
large flathead

1–2 m of 3 kg line

Balance
with
split shot

30 cm

50 cm

Uni or
Locked
Blood
knot

No 8
Swivel

10–15 kg line

**ESTUARY
DRIFT RIG**

Suitable for:
small flathead,
trevally, bream
and snapper

Uni or Locked
Blood knot

15 kg leader

No 2–4
bean sinker

No 1–3
bean sinker

No 4–6
Kendall/Kirby
hook

Uni or
Locked
Blood
knot

No 6 Swivel

Uni or
Locked
Blood
knot

No 8–10
Swivel

Uni or
Locked
Blood
knot

Size 1 or 2
ball sinker

8–12
longshank
hook

Uni or Locked
Blood knot

15–25 kg trace
40–50 cm

30–45 cm

**LIGHT FLOAT
RIG**

Suitable for:
garfish, mullet, yellowtail
and tommy ruff

3/0 to 4/0
ganged hooks

3/0 to 4/0
ganged hooks

Uni or Locked
Blood knot

No 2 to 1/0 hook

RIGS FOR ESTUARY AND BAY FISHING

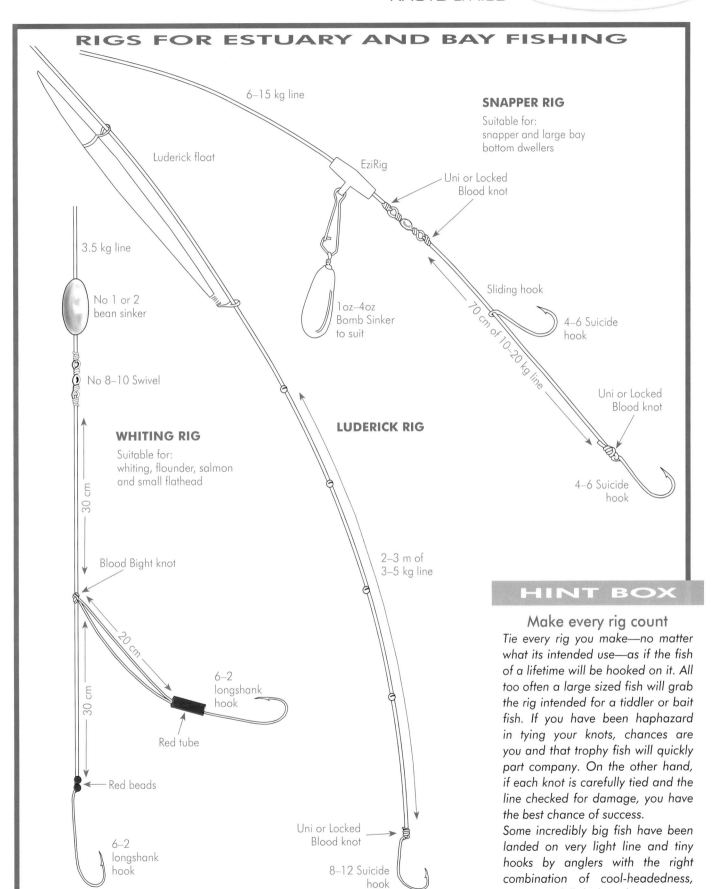

6–15 kg line

Luderick float

EziRig

SNAPPER RIG

Suitable for:
snapper and large bay
bottom dwellers

Uni or Locked
Blood knot

3.5 kg line

No 1 or 2
bean sinker

1oz–4oz
Bomb Sinker
to suit

Sliding hook

70 cm of 10–20 kg line

4–6 Suicide
hook

No 8–10 Swivel

Uni or Locked
Blood knot

WHITING RIG

Suitable for:
whiting, flounder, salmon
and small flathead

LUDERICK RIG

4–6 Suicide
hook

30 cm

Blood Bight knot

20 cm

6–2
longshank
hook

Red tube

2–3 m of
3–5 kg line

30 cm

Red beads

6–2
longshank
hook

Uni or Locked
Blood knot

8–12 Suicide
hook

HINT BOX

Make every rig count

Tie every rig you make—no matter what its intended use—as if the fish of a lifetime will be hooked on it. All too often a large sized fish will grab the rig intended for a tiddler or bait fish. If you have been haphazard in tying your knots, chances are you and that trophy fish will quickly part company. On the other hand, if each knot is carefully tied and the line checked for damage, you have the best chance of success.

Some incredibly big fish have been landed on very light line and tiny hooks by anglers with the right combination of cool-headedness, patience, skill, luck and attention to detail in their rigging.

RIGS FOR BEACH AND ROCK

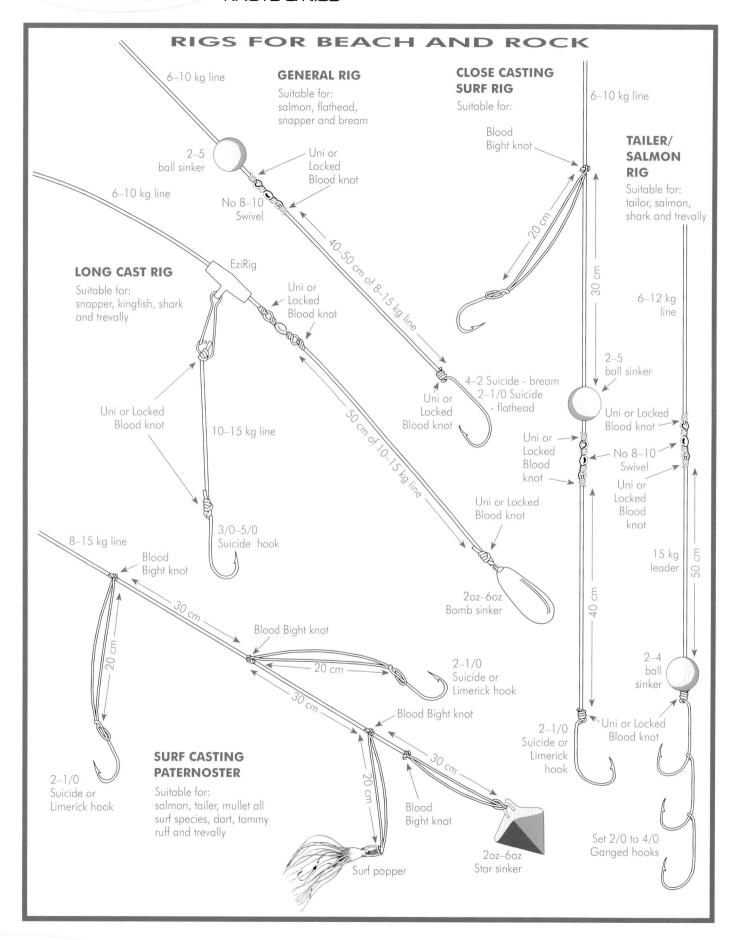

GENERAL RIG
Suitable for:
salmon, flathead,
snapper and bream

6–10 kg line

2–5
ball sinker

Uni or
Locked
Blood knot

6–10 kg line

No 8–10
Swivel

40–50 cm of 8–15 kg line

**CLOSE CASTING
SURF RIG**
Suitable for:

6–10 kg line

Blood
Bight knot

20 cm

**TAILER/
SALMON
RIG**
Suitable for:
tailor, salmon,
shark and trevally

30 cm

6–12 kg
line

2–5
ball sinker

Uni or Locked
Blood knot

No 8–10
Swivel

Uni or
Locked
Blood
knot

15 kg
leader

LONG CAST RIG
Suitable for:
snapper, kingfish, shark
and trevally

EziRig

Uni or
Locked
Blood knot

Uni or Locked
Blood knot

10–15 kg line

50 cm of 10–15 kg line

3/0–5/0
Suicide hook

Uni or
Locked
Blood knot

4–2 Suicide - bream
2–1/0 Suicide
- flathead

Uni or Locked
Blood knot

2oz–6oz
Bomb sinker

40 cm

50 cm

2–4
ball
sinker

8–15 kg line

Blood
Bight knot

30 cm

20 cm

Blood Bight knot

20 cm

2–1/0
Suicide or
Limerick hook

Blood Bight knot

30 cm

30 cm

20 cm

Blood
Bight knot

**SURF CASTING
PATERNOSTER**
Suitable for:
salmon, tailer, mullet all
surf species, dart, tommy
ruff and trevally

2–1/0
Suicide or
Limerick hook

Surf popper

2oz–6oz
Star sinker

2–1/0
Suicide or
Limerick
hook

Uni or Locked
Blood knot

Set 2/0 to 4/0
Ganged hooks

RIGS FOR PIER FISHING

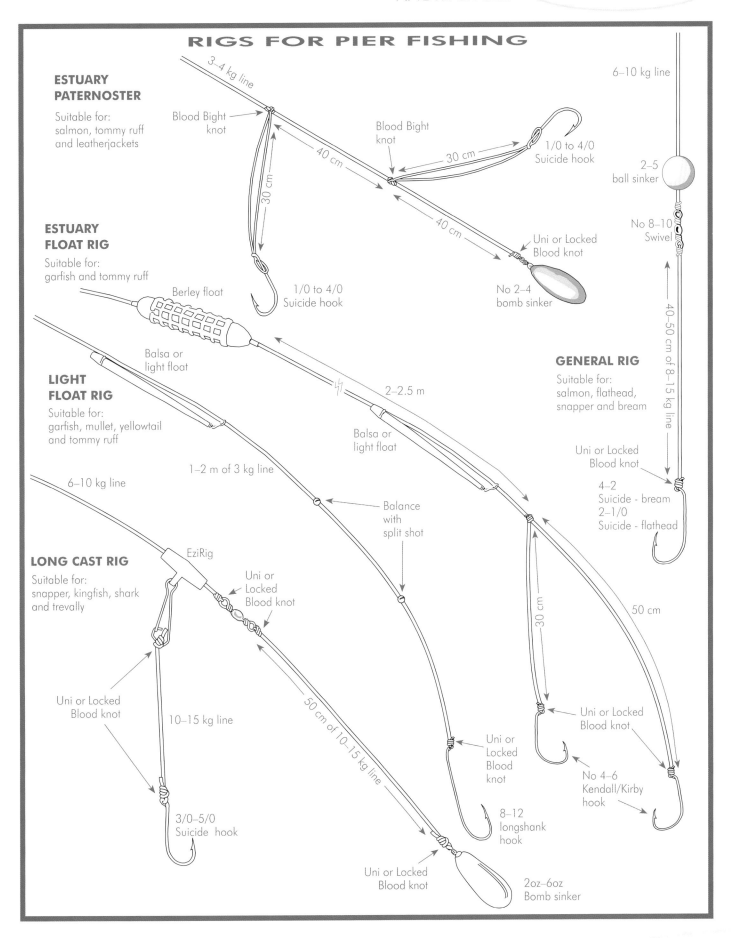

ESTUARY PATERNOSTER

Suitable for: salmon, tommy ruff and leatherjackets

3–4 kg line

Blood Bight knot

Blood Bight knot

40 cm

30 cm

30 cm

1/0 to 4/0 Suicide hook

Uni or Locked Blood knot

40 cm

No 2–4 bomb sinker

1/0 to 4/0 Suicide hook

ESTUARY FLOAT RIG

Suitable for: garfish and tommy ruff

Berley float

Balsa or light float

LIGHT FLOAT RIG

Suitable for: garfish, mullet, yellowtail and tommy ruff

2–2.5 m

Balsa or light float

1–2 m of 3 kg line

6–10 kg line

Balance with split shot

LONG CAST RIG

Suitable for: snapper, kingfish, shark and trevally

EziRig

Uni or Locked Blood knot

Uni or Locked Blood knot

10–15 kg line

50 cm of 10–15 kg line

3/0–5/0 Suicide hook

Uni or Locked Blood knot

8–12 longshank hook

Uni or Locked Blood knot

2oz–6oz Bomb sinker

6–10 kg line

2–5 ball sinker

No 8–10 Swivel

40–50 cm of 8–15 kg line

GENERAL RIG

Suitable for: salmon, flathead, snapper and bream

Uni or Locked Blood knot

4–2 Suicide - bream
2–1/0 Suicide - flathead

30 cm

50 cm

Uni or Locked Blood knot

No 4–6 Kendall/Kirby hook

31

RIGS FOR INSHORE AND OFFSHORE

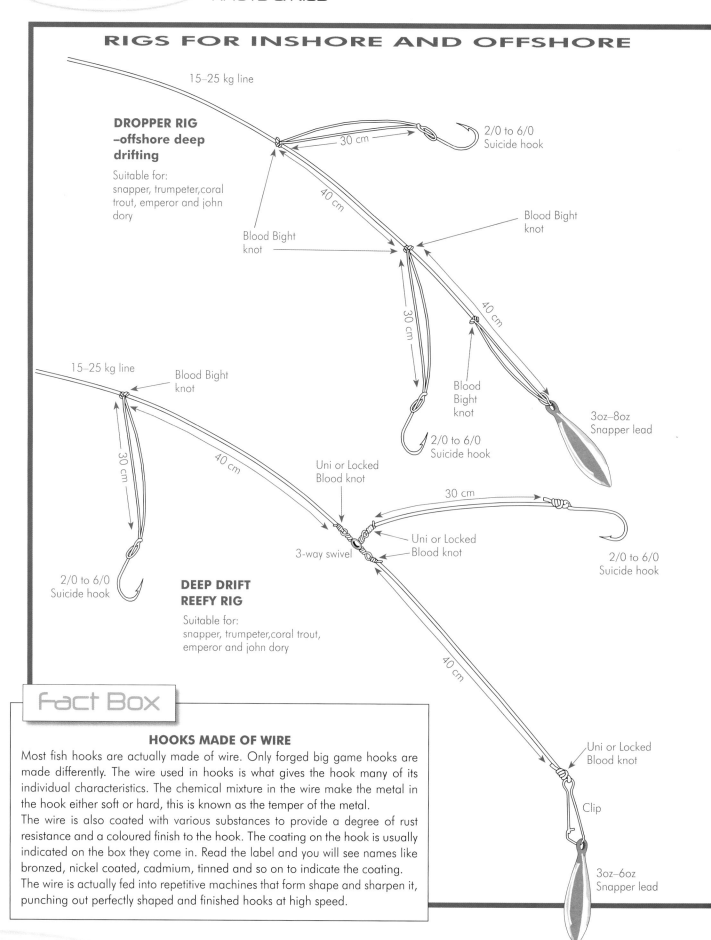

15–25 kg line

**DROPPER RIG
–offshore deep drifting**

Suitable for:
snapper, trumpeter, coral trout, emperor and john dory

Blood Bight knot

30 cm

40 cm

2/0 to 6/0 Suicide hook

Blood Bight knot

30 cm

40 cm

Blood Bight knot

2/0 to 6/0 Suicide hook

3oz–8oz Snapper lead

15–25 kg line

Blood Bight knot

30 cm

40 cm

Uni or Locked Blood knot

3-way swivel

Uni or Locked Blood knot

30 cm

2/0 to 6/0 Suicide hook

2/0 to 6/0 Suicide hook

DEEP DRIFT REEFY RIG

Suitable for:
snapper, trumpeter, coral trout, emperor and john dory

2/0 to 6/0 Suicide hook

40 cm

Uni or Locked Blood knot

Clip

3oz–6oz Snapper lead

fact Box

HOOKS MADE OF WIRE

Most fish hooks are actually made of wire. Only forged big game hooks are made differently. The wire used in hooks is what gives the hook many of its individual characteristics. The chemical mixture in the wire make the metal in the hook either soft or hard, this is known as the temper of the metal.

The wire is also coated with various substances to provide a degree of rust resistance and a coloured finish to the hook. The coating on the hook is usually indicated on the box they come in. Read the label and you will see names like bronzed, nickel coated, cadmium, tinned and so on to indicate the coating.

The wire is actually fed into repetitive machines that form shape and sharpen it, punching out perfectly shaped and finished hooks at high speed.

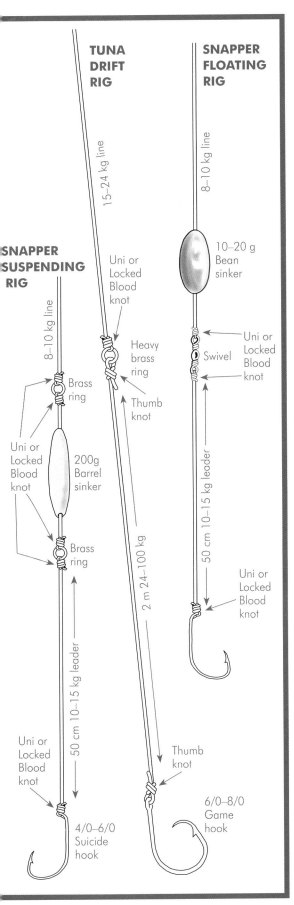

TUNA DRIFT RIG

15–24 kg line

Uni or Locked Blood knot

Heavy brass ring

Thumb knot

2 m 24–100 kg

Thumb knot

6/0–8/0 Game hook

SNAPPER FLOATING RIG

8–10 kg line

10–20 g Bean sinker

Uni or Locked Blood knot

Swivel

Uni or Locked Blood knot

50 cm 10–15 kg leader

Uni or Locked Blood knot

SNAPPER SUSPENDING RIG

8–10 kg line

Brass ring

Uni or Locked Blood knot

200g Barrel sinker

Brass ring

50 cm 10–15 kg leader

Uni or Locked Blood knot

4/0–6/0 Suicide hook

UNITS OF MEASURE

Everyone knows that Australia's official way of measuring length, weight etc is with the metric system. This is a simple system where units are given in multiples of ten and changes in units (for example, from grams to kilograms) are also in multiples of ten. However, this has not always been the case and many countries still have not adopted the metric system.

The system that was used in Australia and is still used in many countries—most notably in the United States of America—is the imperial system. This system uses pounds and ounces for weight, and feet and inches for length. Many older anglers were brought up using the imperial system and still refer to their equipment in those terms, so if you get advice then much of it may be in those terms.

Historically the imperial weights set some targets that anglers used as milestones to aim for. A ten pound trout was, and still is, considered a tremendous capture, while a 4.5 kg (or even 5 kg) trout doesn't have the same attraction. Similarly a thirty pound snapper, or a hundred pound Murray cod or mulloway is a fish that remains in an angler's memory forever.

Many items of fishing equipment are also measured, used and sold using imperial measurements. Most lures and jigs that are used with soft plastics are sold as fractions of an ounce. Sinkers too are usually refereed to in ounces—beach anglers' are usually 2, 4 or 6 ounces rather than 50, 100 or 150 grams. Fly anglers have always used feet and inches to measure the length of their rods, rarely referring to them in metric terms. A 9 ft fly rod is the classic average length of their rods and leaders vary from six to eighteen feet.

So as you increase your fishing experience you will need to be familiar with both the metric and imperial measurement systems and it is very handy to be able to quickly convert between the two. A little practice and a trick or two is all that is necessary for most people who have been brought up using the metric system exclusively to enable then to convert to the imperial measurements.

CONVERSION FACTORS

Weight

1 ounce = 28.4 grams
1 pound = 454 grams

10 grams = 0.35 ounces
1 kilogram = 2.205 pounds

(To convert from kilograms to pounds quickly and approximately, double the number of pounds and then add a tenth of that number to itself.)

Length

1 inch = 2.54 cm
1 foot = 30.5 cm

1 cm = 0.4 inches
1 metre = 39.4 inches

(To convert from inches to centimetres quickly and approximately, multiply the number of inches by ten and divide the result by four.)

Conversion tables

Here are some tables to help you to convert between the metric and imperial systems.

LB	KG
1	0.5
2	0.9
3	1.4
4	1.8
5	2.3
6	2.7
7	3.2
8	3.6
9	4.1
10	4.5
15	6.8
20	9.1
25	11.4
30	13.6
40	18.2
50	22.7
60	27.2
70	31.8
80	36.3
90	40.9
100	45.4

KG	LB
0.5	1.1
1	2.2
2	4.4
3	6.6
4	8.8
5	11.0
6	13.2
7	15.4
8	17.6
9	19.8
10	22.0
15	33.0
20	44.1
30	66.1
40	88.1
50	110.1
60	132.2
70	154.2
80	176.2
90	198.2
100	220.3

OZ	Grams
1/32	0.9
1/16	0.2
1/8	3.5
3/16	5.3
1/4	7.1
3/8	10.6
1/2	14.2
5/8	17.7
3/4	21.3
1	28.4
1 1/4	35.4
1 1/2	42.5
2	56.7
3	85
4	113
6	170
8	227
12	340
16	454

IN	CM
10	25.4
11	27.9
12	30.5
13	33.0
14	35.6
15	38.1
16	40.6
17	43.2
18	45.7
19	48.3
20	50.8
25	63.5
30	76.2
40	101.6
50	127.0
60	152.4
70	177.8
80	203.2
90	228.6
100	254.0
120	304.8
150	381.0

CM	IN
20	7.9
21	8.3
22	8.7
23	9.1
24	9.4
25	9.8
26	10.2
27	10.6
28	11.0
29	11.4
30	11.8
35	13.8
40	15.7
45	17.7
50	19.7
60	23.6
70	27.6
80	31.5
90	35.4
100	39.4
120	47.2
150	59.1

RIGS FOR FRESHWATER FISHING

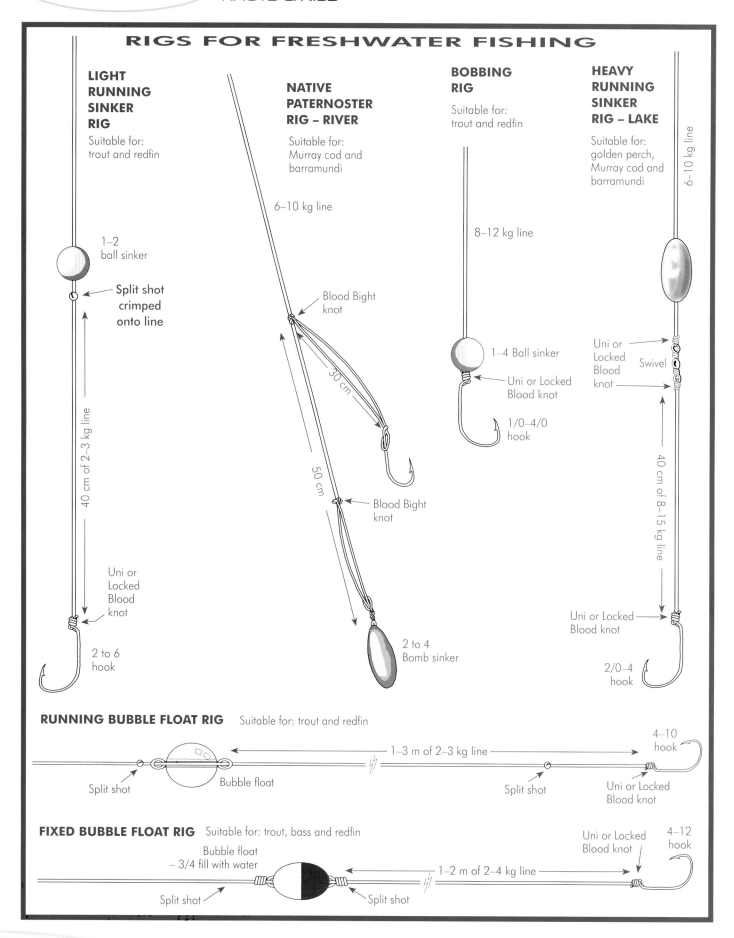

LIGHT RUNNING SINKER RIG

Suitable for: trout and redfin

1–2 ball sinker

Split shot crimped onto line

40 cm of 2–3 kg line

Uni or Locked Blood knot

2 to 6 hook

NATIVE PATERNOSTER RIG – RIVER

Suitable for: Murray cod and barramundi

6–10 kg line

Blood Bight knot

30 cm

50 cm

Blood Bight knot

2 to 4 Bomb sinker

BOBBING RIG

Suitable for: trout and redfin

8–12 kg line

1–4 Ball sinker

Uni or Locked Blood knot

1/0–4/0 hook

HEAVY RUNNING SINKER RIG – LAKE

Suitable for: golden perch, Murray cod and barramundi

6–10 kg line

Uni or Locked Blood knot Swivel

40 cm of 8–15 kg line

Uni or Locked Blood knot

2/0–4 hook

RUNNING BUBBLE FLOAT RIG Suitable for: trout and redfin

Split shot

Bubble float

1–3 m of 2–3 kg line

Split shot

4–10 hook

Uni or Locked Blood knot

FIXED BUBBLE FLOAT RIG Suitable for: trout, bass and redfin

Bubble float – 3/4 fill with water

Split shot

Split shot

1–2 m of 2–4 kg line

Uni or Locked Blood knot

4–12 hook

SALTWATER HOOK GUIDE

BAIT	HOOK MODEL	SIZE
BREAD DOUGH	SNECK	8–12
CRAB LIGHT	SUICIDE	1/0–2
CUNJEVOI	VIKING	2/0–1
CUT BAIT	SUICIDE	3/0–1/0
MULLET (PODDY) LIVE	KIRBY	1/0–3/0
NIPPERS	BAITHOLDER	1/0–2
OCTOPUS/SQUID	SUICIDE	5/0–2/0
PILCHARD	GANGED HOOKS	3/0–4/0
PILCHARD	SUICIDE	5/0–2/0

BAIT	HOOK MODEL	SIZE
PIPI/COCKLE	BAITHOLDER	8–12
PRAWN	BAITHOLDER	1/0–2
SHRIMP	BAITHOLDER	4–8
WEED	SNECK	8–12
WHITEBAIT	LIGHT SUICIDE	1/0–2
WORM BEACH	EXTRA LONG SHANK	1/0–4
WORM BLOOD	EXTRA LONG SHANK	1/0–4
YELLOWTAIL LIVE	LIVE BAIT HOOK	4/0–8/0

FRESHWATER HOOK GUIDE

BAIT	HOOK MODEL	SIZE
ARTIFICIAL (eg. Powerbait)	BAITHOLDER	4–8
CRICKETS & GRASSHOPPERS	LONGSHANK	1–4
FISH (minnows, smelt,galaxids)	SUICIDE	1–4
GRUBS	BAITHOLDER	2/0–2
MAGGOTS	BAITHOLDER	8–12

BAIT	HOOK MODEL	SIZE
MUDEYES	SLICED SUICIDE	6–12
SHRIMP	BAITHOLDER	6–8
WORMS SCRUB	SUICIDE	2–6
WORMS GARDEN	BAITHOLDER	4–8
YABBY	VIKING	8–12

CHAPTER 4

BAIT

The bait you use and how you present it will have a big effect on what type and how many fish you catch. Bait can come from a range of sources. You can buy it from a shop, you can catch it yourself and you can even make some of it at home. The important thing to remember about bait is that it must appeal as a food item to the fish you want to catch.

Part of the problem when you start fishing is that there is so much choice and so many different ways to catch the fish. Prawns, pilchards, whitebait, squid, gut bait, worms and some shellfish are available at the tackle shop. Although you can catch some of these yourself, the shop is usually where most anglers get these types of bait.

The best way to start is to choose baits with general appeal that will catch a wide range of fish. The following sets out some of the most popular baits.

PRAWNS AND PRAWNING

Prawns are one of the best all-round baits available, just about everything likes to eat them. They can be fished whole for large fish or you can peel and cut them into small pieces; there is very little waste.

When you buy fresh or frozen prawns always check they are in good condition. The prawns should have a bright, shiny appearance with no black coloration around the head or legs.

Despite the high cost of prawns for both the table and for bait, there are many places where enough prawns can be gathered for bait by any angler keen to spend a few night hours chasing them.

Most estuaries around the country are inhabited by several different species of prawns. The prawns themselves spend all or part of their life cycle in the estuary, with many species completing the adult part of their life by migrating to the open sea. This migration is well known in many coastal towns as the prawn 'run'. These prawn runs occur with the new moon period (no moon present) each month from October to April.

The prawns use the lack of moonlight to help stop fish seeing them during their migration. Anglers seeking the prawns need to consult a tide chart and note the three days either side of the new moon and when the run out tides occur in that period.

While the dark of the moon represents a peak in prawn activity, some prawns (enough for bait) can be found on most nights. All that is needed is the right equipment and to look in the right place.

The best areas to seek prawns are around shallow, tidal sand flats particularly those near mangroves and seagrass beds. The prawns spend much of their time in and

DANGER ALERT **FISH FACT**

BEWARE THE FORTESQUE

Estuary anglers and particularly those chasing prawns will often encounter fortesques. These mottled grey and black members of the scorpion fish family can inflict a painful, firey sting if handled. They only grow to about 55 mm but they turn up in prawn drag nets and are regularly caught when fishing with small hooks for leatherjackets and other bottom fish.

The fortesque has a big cousin too, the bullrout, which looks the same but grows to about 200 mm and it packs a big sting too. Watch out for these fish in your captures. Don't handle anything if you don't know what it is, and always handle these little brutes with pliers.

If you go prawning never run your hands through the catch, always spill it out into a fish box and sort it bit by bit.

around the seagrass beds so this is always a good place to look.

The main prawn producing areas will be well known to local anglers and any fishing tackle shop in the area should be able to tell you where the prawning grounds are located.

Equipment

Dip nets have a relatively small mesh and can catch and hold prawns from small to large sizes. They are easy to carry and store and need only the addition of a strong torch, gas lantern or under water prawn light to enable the capture of prawns or other bait.

The nets work best when used in pairs, with two people walking around the selected area together, each with a light and net. The reason for this is that outside of prawn 'runs' where the prawns are at or near the surface, most of the prawns will be found on the bottom and it may be necessary for two nets to be used, to force the prawn into one net or the other.

During prawn runs, the anglers either stand in the current or sit in a boat anchored across the current. A powerful lantern is then used to illuminate the area and the prawns are scooped up as they travel in the current on their seaward migration. The scooped prawns can be left in the dip net until enough have been collected to return to shore where they are emptied into a lidded bucket, half filled with seawater.

When there are plenty of prawns, the large ones are kept for eating and the small ones for bait. Of course many people just eat them all.

Keeping prawns for bait

The best way to keep the prawns alive once captured is in a container with smaller holes in it, left submerged in seawater. If this is not available they can also be kept in a container like a large bucket or an ice box full of water with an aerator running to keep the oxygen supply going.

If you need to transport the prawns from where you catch them

to another spot where you intend to use them, the best method is in an ice box with plenty of wet seaweed. Temperature control is important, so don't leave the prawns where they will heat up. That is why ice box type storage is preferred. Always store the live prawns in a cool, shady spot.

For quality frozen prawns, place the prawns in one of those shallow, rectangular containers that Chinese take-away comes in. Place a couple of handfuls of prawns in the container, fill with saltwater to cover the prawns and freeze. The prawns will thaw out crisp and without any black around the head or legs.

Good presentation counts

When using prawns as bait always present them as the fish are used to seeing them, straight and flat. Live prawns only need to be lightly hooked through the tail, the fish gulp them down anyway. Dead prawns should be placed on the hook by putting the point of the hook through the anal vent and then bringing the first three body segments onto the hook. This will present an attractive, natural bait.

If you have the opportunity to catch or use prawns live then do so, there are few better baits, and catching the prawns is fun too.

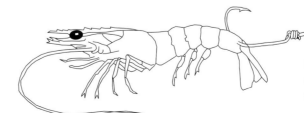

Live prawn presented attractively are irresistable to many fish species

Pilchards and whitebait

Flathead, tailor, salmon, mackerel, trevally, snapper, bream, cod and barracouta all like pilchards and whitebait. The bait fish should look firm and bright. Always look at the stomach cavity area, if this is broken or badly discoloured on the bait fish don't buy them, they are in poor condition.

Whole pilchards or whitebait are best presented on ganged hooks which hold them together really well. On smaller fish, pieces of pilchard or whitebait also work.

Squid

Squid is a good, tough bait. It will stay on the hook when other baits are being easily removed by small fish. However, squid does not have the wide appeal of baits like prawns, so its use is often limited. Bream, mulloway, kingfish, snapper and cod all like squid bait.

Squid come in all shapes and sizes from little bottle squid of a few centimetres up to the massive giant squid of the deep oceans that can be up to 10 metres long. Once a part of mythology, giant squid have now been filmed and a few good specimens have been captured for scientific study.

Squid are great fun to catch and can be found in both the estuaries and offshore. They regularly turn up around piers and wharves, weedbeds, kelp areas, rocky headlands and shallow offshore reefs.

Squid have a very short life cycle with almost all species living about one year or just a little more, even the giants. This probably accounts for their voracious appetites and aggressive hunting.

Weed

Blackfish are a very popular angling fish but they mostly eat seaweed rather than more standard baits. Anglers can either buy this weed from the tackle shop or learn to collect it around shallow bays.

The weed is placed on the hook by bending a loop of it around the top of the hook and then cris-crossing back down the hook. This holds it securely in place for the fish to bite.

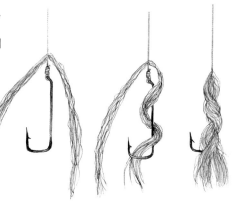

Worms

Various species of worms are sold at bait shops and although expensive, live worms make great bait. Blood worms, beachworms, tube worms and wrigglers are all sold at times.

Make sure you store the worms in a cool place to keep them alive.

Freshwater anglers can buy a variety of earthworms and scrubworms, and these are very good bait.

Gut bait

Both mullet gut and chicken gut are available in many bait shops and they are good bait for bream. They do smell a bit though, so always clean your hands after putting it on the hook. Always keep gut baits on ice or out of the sun until you are ready to use it as it can go rotten very quickly.

Dough

Dough is a simple mixture of flour and water, which is beaten with a fork or spoon until it has a firm texture that can be easily moulded into a little shape and put on a hook. Dough is used to catch mullet, garfish, yellowtail, bream and other small fish. The important part is to get the consistency just right so it is easy to use when out fishing—not too runny and not too crumbly.

Bread

Bread can be used in several different ways. The crust will usually sit quite well on a hook and makes a good bait while the centre of really fresh bread can be easily worked into doughy pellets or the bread can be wet and kneaded into a doughy mix that will stay on a hook.

Minced steak

Raw minced steak will be taken by several species of fish. It is mostly used as bait for yellowtail and other small jetty species.

Steak

Strips of skirt or blade steak are used by bream anglers. The steak can also be cut into very small pieces for use on wharf species.

'Pudding'

Pudding baits are used by bream anglers with great success. A pudding is really any concoction that is made

from bread, flour, finely chopped garlic sausage, cheese and other bits and pieces. The ingredients are mixed together until it has a firm consistency. It is formed into a teardrop shape and put on the hook for use.

GATHERING YOUR OWN BAIT

Gathering and catching your own bait is often as much fun as catching the fish. It not only saves you money, but it also means having the freshest bait possible when you go fishing.

Saltwater yabbies

These burrowing shrimp of the coastal sand flats are a prized bait as almost all fish relish their soft, succulent flesh. Yabbies have one large claw and are also called 'bass yabby' in Victoria and 'pink nipper' in NSW. The term nipper is right—they can nip you with that large claw so handle them carefully.

Yabbies live in the sandbanks of nearly all coastal estuaries and are located by telltale round holes surrounded by a raised collar. They tend to colonise a favoured area with many thousands of shrimp living in any particular sandbank.

A bait pump is used to suck these

little shrimp out of the mud and the pump then empty them onto the sand, where they are collected and placed in a bucket of clean seawater. Yabbies work best when used live, so change the water when you finish pumping and store the bucket in a cool place until you use them.

Shrimps

Small shrimp can be found in weedbeds in most estuaries and can be caught by running a fine mesh net, similar to a butterfly net, through the ribbon weed. A prawn scoop net can be used, but put a handful of seaweed in the end of the net to prevent the shrimp escaping through the mesh. The shrimp can then be kept alive in a bucket of seawater.

When using the shrimp for bait, use small hooks like a No. 8 or No. 10. Despite their small size the shrimp are really attractive to fish like whiting, flounder, leatherjackets, bream and flathead.

Fact Box

DIFFERENCE BETWEEN A FRESH AND SALTWATER YABBY

Apart from both being crustaceans and both making excellent baits, these two creatures have little in common. The saltwater yabby, which is also called a bass yabby, pink nipper, ghost prawn or clicker, is a small, pinkish white, prawn-like creature with one oversized claw. It lives in burrows on tidal sand flats and is usually taken by anglers using a specially designed suction device called a bait pump.

On the other hand, the freshwater yabby, actually several different species, grows considerably larger than its marine counterpart, has two well developed claws, is usually brown, dark blue or black and can most readily be captured on a line baited with meat or in a baited trap

Above are two saltwater yabbies each with the one exaggerated claw as compared with the freshwater yabby below showing two even claws.

Crabs and green nippers

Small crabs and a shrimp known as a green nipper can be found by turning over rocks, particularly those close to the low tide mark. Just remember to put the rocks back in place once you have caught your bait, lots of other little animals live there.

Little crabs and green nippers make great bait for all sorts of fish and they are easy to catch. Just collect enough for bait, don't take too many.

Crabs make very good bream bait

Worms

Worms such as blood and wriggler worms can be dug in many estuaries and beach worms can be caught on ocean beaches. Digging worms is hard work but if you know an area where worms can be dug you have a great bait supply available.

Beach worms can be caught on east coast surf beaches using your fingers or special plastic pliers. This takes a bit of practice but young anglers can learn to catch them faster than adults—all it takes is concentration and patience.

The worm is attracted to the surface by a fish head waved through the wash and the worm's head will be seen arching through the receding wash. The worm is then offered a pipi tongue, which it will grip. The worm is then drawn slightly from the sand and the head gripped with either the fingers or worm pliers. Once the

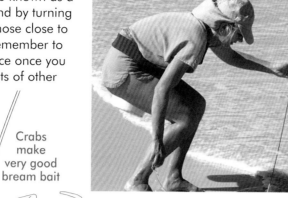

Catching beachworms takes a lot of concentration but can be wet and wild fun.

angler has hold of the worm it is drawn from the sand. Some beach worms can be 2 metres long.

Catching beach worms is wet and wild fun and after a while you will be able to collect plenty of them.

Small fish

Small fish make great bait for larger predatory fish. These can be captured in a variety of ways.

Plastic bait traps are handy and can be baited with bread and placed in the sh allows to catch mullet, sprats and herring. Many small fish can also be caught in general fishing by using a light line with a small split shot and a little hook. This is baited with a piece of prawn or strip of fish flesh. Small fish can also be caught using a prawn scoop net and a bright light at night.

Peeled prawn

Bait jigs are also very useful for catching a wide range of small and not so small baitfish.

Bait jigs (Sabiki rigs)

Bait jigs are one of the most effective fish catching devices ever invented. Also known as the Sabiki jig rig, the bait jig is used to catch a wide variety of fish species from tiny bait fish to quite sizeable table fish. The jigs are popular because of their simplicity

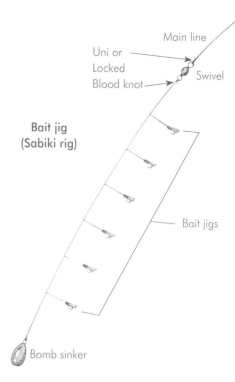

Main line

Uni or Locked
Blood knot

Swivel

Bait jig (Sabiki rig)

Bait jigs

Bomb sinker

and their devastating effectiveness on the fish.

What are bait jigs?
Bait jigs are sets of small, white, pearl or pink coloured flies attached to small droppers along a length of relatively heavy monofilament line with a swivel at one end. Each complete packaged rig usually carries four to six flies and is about 1.2 m long. The six hooks and the length of the jig can be awkward and unwieldily to use, particularly if the fish are thick or the angler finds the rig too long to handle comfortably. The answer is to cut the jig in half. It will be just as effective and much easier to handle.

Bait jigs also help those new to the

Fact Box   DANGER ALERT

WARNING
There is only one problem with bait jigs, the hooks are really sharp and the combination of struggling little fish and lots of free swinging hooks has seen plenty of people firmly hooked in either the hand or the face. So take care when using these jigs. If you are just starting out, use half a jig, they work just as well and are much easier to handle.

sport as there are no complex rigs or knots, you just tie them on and they work.

How to rig them

To rig a bait jig, attach your main line to the swivel provided. Then tie a sinker, usually fairly heavy to the other end. The sinker provides weight to work the jig up and down through the water layers.

One important point with the bait jigs is that they are manufactured so the little flies actually 'stand off' the main line. This bias will only work if you attach the jigs the right way up. To check this, hold the jig one way up then the other. The way that has the flies standing off the trace is the right way up.

How they're sold

Bait jigs can be purchased at most tackle stores and cost between $2 and $4 each, depending on their size and style. They come in a range of hook sizes with the correct selection being based on what size fish or bait is being sought. Generally the smaller hook sizes (No. 10 or 8) are the best all round performers, but for larger fish like slimy mackerel or trevally size No. 4 would be a good choice.

How they work

The success of bait jigs is reliant as much on the actual jig design itself as it is on the method used to fish them. In reality, these small jigs or flies are actually mini lures and they need to be given action by the angler to be productive.

Bait jigs should be fished with a slow jigging action, by lifting the rod up and dropping the rod tip down at the end of the lift. In deeper water this lift and drop technique can have a slow retrieve added to work the lure through various water levels. Once the level at which the bait is feeding has been established the jig should be lowered to that point and jigged up and down.

Often when one fish hooks up, its struggling will excite the other fish around it and all the available hooks will have a fish on them. Once you hook a fish don't keep jigging, if you do you will end up with a massive tangle. Just wind the fish in.

Bait jigs can also be 'spiced' by putting a pinch of prawn or a small strip of fish on each hook. This can really help to get the fish biting if they are a bit shy to take the jigs. Berley also helps to concentrate the fish for you and encourages them to bite.

Shellfish

Shellfish like pipis, mussels, cockles and razor shells can be found on beaches, mudflats and rock shelves. These shellfish are all good bait and can be easily harvested and used in fishing.

They appeal most to bottom feeding fish like bream, whiting, leatherjackets and trevally.

Most of these shellfish need to be opened with a knife, so take care when doing this. Some shellfish baits can be soft and difficult to hold on a hook so care must be taken both in their attachment and when casting.

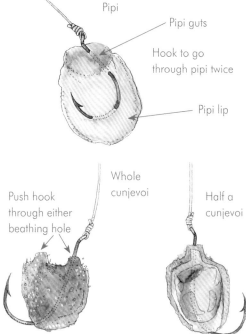

Pipi

Pipi guts

Hook to go through pipi twice

Pipi lip

Push hook through either beathing hole

Whole cunjevoi

Half a cunjevoi

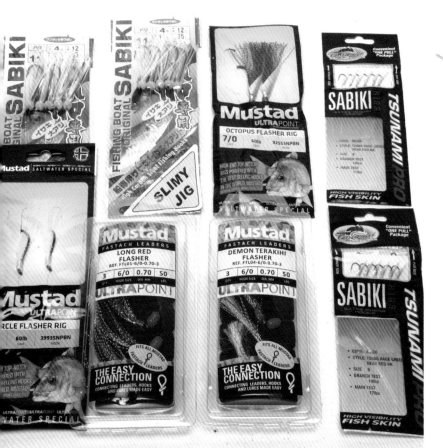

LEFT: A range of bait jigs is available at most tackle shops.

CHAPTER 5

BERLEY

The purpose of berley is to attract fish to a particular area and to make them bite more actively. It plays a vital roll in angling and most successful anglers use berley as part of their fishing strategy.

WHAT IS BERLEY?

Berley can be anything that is attractive to the fish you seek. For jetty anglers fishing for mullet, garfish, yellowtail, tommy ruff or slimy mackerel well soaked bread finely pulped is excellent. Soaked chicken pellets or dog biscuits also work well on fish like bream, trevally and carp. Mashed potato, soaked wheat, bran, pollard, stale biscuits, stale breakfast cereal and virtually anything else that can be pulped can be used to make a berley mix.

Offshore anglers seeking kingfish or yellowfin tuna might use pilchards chopped into sections or tuna or mullet pulped in a berley bucket attached to the boat.

Whatever is used, it must be attractive to the fish and it must be delivered in such a way that it works in your fishing area and does not just drift away uselessly.

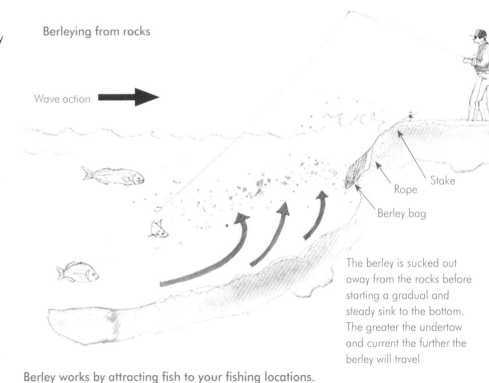

Berleying from rocks

Wave action

Stake

Rope

Berley bag

The berley is sucked out away from the rocks before starting a gradual and steady sink to the bottom. The greater the undertow and current the further the berley will travel

Berley works by attracting fish to your fishing locations.

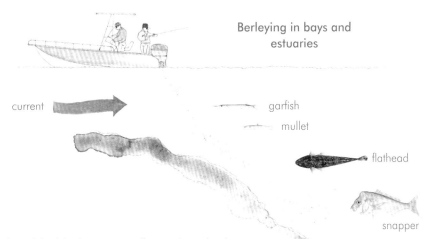

Berleying in bays and
estuaries

current

garfish

mullet

flathead

snapper

Finely mulched berley is more effective than chunky
berley in attracting fish. The idea is to have a fine 'mist' of berley
dispersing away from your position in a boat or on the shore so that fish
are attracted by being made to feel hungry but are unable to fill themselves up
on it. A light current is necessary to carry the berley to distant fish whether they
are swimming in mid-water or on the bottom.

Making berley

Some berley is simple with things like a loaf of bread soaked in a bucket of water to produce a pulpy mixture. By squeezing this mixture in your hand just before throwing it into the water you remove most of the air trapped inside the bread. This allows the bread to sink and will quickly attract surface and mid water fish.

If you need berley on the bottom, for fish like bream, trevally or snapper, you can make berley bombs at home to take fishing with you. Berley bombs are usually made with wet bread, chopped pilchards or other fish scraps or a tin of sardines

WATCH THE CURRENT
The current or tide will have a big effect on your berley and how it attracts the fish. In strong current, the berley can be carried away quickly and serve little purpose. Berley works best when it stays fairly close to where you're fishing.

The actual weight and type of berley will also affect how it reacts in the current. Lightweight berley like soaked bread drifts away quickly, while chicken pellets, dog biscuits or chopped pilchards sink quickly.

So when you want to use berley, always check what the current or tide is going to do with the berley. You can then adjust your cast or bait presentation to suit where the fish are most likely gathering to eat the berley.

all mixed together with wet sand.

The mixture is worked into a firm consistency so the sand can be shaped into balls or it can just be placed in used plastic fast food containers. The wet mixture is then

Powerful Smells

Berley can be improved by adding substances that have powerful smells. Fish, like most animals have a very good sense of smell and all sorts of things can help get them biting.

You can add tuna oil to almost any berley or you can add the oil from a can of sardines to your berley. You can either eat the sardines or use them in the berley too. Chopped pilchards also have a lot of oil in them and a strong smell, which helps make the mixture more inviting. Some companies even produce additives for berley. You just put the recommended number of drops in the berley mix and the additive leaves an attractive smell in the berley.

Mullet attracted by bread berley gather, waiting for the next handful.

FISH FACT

FLYING FISH

Until you actually see a flying fish take off from beside the boat it's hard to understand just how a fish can fly. Coloured brilliant blue on top and silver underneath and about the size of an average mullet they streak out of the ocean, wings spread and tail beating furiously. They use the wind for lift and in good conditions they can rise about 3 to 4 metres and then glide for 60 or 70 metres, before folding their wings as they splashdown.

Flying fish use this spectacular piece of evolutionary adaptation to evade their predators.

left in the freezer until it is needed. When you go fishing, the frozen 'bombs' are dropped into the water every 20 minutes or so. Being mostly sand they sink fast and being frozen, they thaw out gradually releasing their attractive mixture right in the fishing area.

Additives

The addition of tuna oil to most berley mixes seems to add to their attractiveness, as does the addition of finely chopped pilchards or sardines. Tuna oil is an essential additive to berley used for tommy ruff. Tuna oil can be bought from most tackle shops.

Berley floats

Also known as feeder floats, these are cigar shaped, plastic cages with holes along the side. The cage is loaded with

the berley mixture and cast into the fishing area. The hook or hooks are usually attached close to the feeder float so the baited hook remains right in the middle of the berley stream being released from the feeder float.

When to berley

You should start berleying as soon as you arrive at the selected fishing spot or drop anchor. The berley should be added every few minutes until the fish start biting. Once the fish are attracted and start biting, the berley stream should be reduced but continued to keep them interested in feeding.

Drawn by the berley, fish mill around waiting for more.

Adding berley to the water at a jetty, especially at the change of the tide, can bring the fish on to the bite.

CHAPTER 6

LURES

Lures are artificial baits designed to attract fish and work because they look like or move like a small fish, crustacean or other object that larger fish like to eat. The huge numbers of lures displayed at tackle shops can be confusing but all you need to do is buy a lure you can cast easily and that resembles the sort of bait you would use for the type of fish you are after.

Selecting Lures

Lure casting is one of the best ways to catch a fish and you should always keep a range of lures in your kit or tackle box. There are thousands of different lures to choose from, but it is best when starting out to choose a selection of 'all-round' styles and colours. Select a range of lures that will work in both salt and fresh water and on a wide variety of different fish species.

Even though there are thousands of lures on the tackle shop walls they essentially come in the following classifications: plugs & minnows, spoons, slices & wobblers, soft plastics, surface poppers, spinners, spinnerblades or spinnerbaits, skirted trolling lures and bibless minnows. Lures for salt water species need to be a bit heavier and stronger than their freshwater counterparts, but there are many that will do both jobs, especially in the crossover between freshwater, estuary and light saltwater.

For instance, the classic spoon, the Wonder Wobbler is one of the most universal lures produced in Australia and will catch fish across the spectrum, on all species in salt and fresh water. The Rapala CD Minnow range is yet another classic that can be cast or trolled and is a lure that will catch just about anything that swims including trout, salmon and tuna. One of the most versatile diving plugs about is the StumpJumper and comes with the added advantage that each lure has a selection of three different and replaceable bibs, these mean that you can vary the action and dive depth of the lure by simply changing the bib.

Strategies

Where you fish, what lure you chose and whether you retrieve it along the bottom, in mid-water or along the surface will dictate the type of fish you are likely to catch.

If you fish in Sydney Harbour the most likely fish you will catch on lures is tailor. They really go for small, silver fish so a silver spoon or slice trolled or cast and retrieved mid-water is a good choice.

If you fish around areas like in Port Phillip Bay that have lots of flathead on the bottom, then a soft plastic jig bounced along the bottom will be eaten with gusto.

In northern tropical waters where there are lots of lure-eating fish, you should choose a standard minnow-type lure that looks like a small mullet or herring. The lure should also be easy to cast and you'll catch a range of fish from barra to mangrove jack.

If freshwater fishing in lakes then trolling a Tassie Devil just below the surface in open water will most likely pick up a rainbow trout, but if you troll closer to shore near where the water shallows then it is more likely to catch a brown trout.

The list goes on and on but the basic principles remain the same, match the lure with the food of the target species and place it where you expect the fish to be waiting.

Presentation

Once you have a lure that the fish in your area like to eat, the next consideration is presentation. Some anglers believe that it is more important than what the lure looks like. It is important to use the lure where the fish are most likely to be feeding. Just casting a lure around aimlessly does not catch many fish.

Fish that feed in open water, like tailor, salmon and trevally, might be located with random casting, but even these fish can be targeted more specifically. When seeking open water fish, always look for tide lines, points or jetties that drop into deeper water or for signs of the fish feeding on small fry. This may be marked by splashes or birds feeding over a working school of fish.

Fish like bass, barramundi, Murray cod and many others will be found close to snags, fallen trees, mangrove roots and the mouth of small creeks that join a main river.

River trout tend to feed at the top and bottom of pools or along undercut banks.

Flathead work the channel edges, drop-offs and the edges of weedbeds.

Knowing this information is the key to lure fishing. By putting a lure that resembles something the fish likes to eat very close to where the fish lives you are most likely to be rewarded with a crashing strike.

Speed kills

Speed is a vital ingredient in lure fishing. Once you cast the lure it needs to be retrieved at a speed that is attractive to the fish. The lure speed and its action are what induce the fish to strike. Fast feeding fish like tuna and bonito need a fast retrieve, fish that dwell near snags usually need a slower, more active presentation.

Watch the lure you use carefully and check that you are retrieving it at a rate that makes it look attractive in the water.

It might seem a bit difficult at first but once you get the general idea and know how the lure should work then things improve rapidly from there. You can add to the lure's action by small, rapid twitches of the rod tip as you retrieve the lure.

Trolling or casting

Lures can be presented by either trolling or casting—it depends on your situation.

Trolling is done from a boat or canoe with the boat's speed matching the feeding speed of the fish being sought and the swimming action of the lure being used. Trolling is very productive on open water fish such as tuna, bonito, kingfish, trevally, tailor, salmon and barracouta. It is also very effective on dams for trout and native fish. Clever trolling can also be used to work lures around snags and other likely spots by using the boat to position the lures where fish are likely to be feeding.

Casting is usually more selective, with the angler choosing the target area and working the lure to attract a strike. Casting can be great fun, as you will often see the fish attacking the lure, which adds to the thrill.

When casting lures you need to develop your accuracy so you can place the lure where it is most likely to be attacked by the fish. Accuracy comes with practice so don't worry if some of the casts don't land in exactly the right spot at first. If you don't snag up the lure occasionally then you're probably not putting the lure in the best place for the fish.

Plugs & minnows

These are by far the most popular lures and come in hundreds of different shapes, sizes and diving configurations. They can float, sink or suspend and, depending on the size and shape of the bib, they can dive to depths of up to 10 metres. Many of these lures are only at their best as either a casting lure or as a trolling lure, but there are a few that will perform equally well in both forms of presentation. Such lures include the Nilsmaster Invincible range, the Rapala CD and Husky Jerk range, the RMG Scorpion range and the Predatek Boomerang range.

Small minnows like the Rapala CD5 and the Rebel Craw are terrific lures to troll and cast for trout. The McGrath diving minnow is a classic trolling diving minnow lure that will catch trout, bass and other native fish, while the Deception Nipper is a classic casting lure for the same species.

Up north there are dozens of

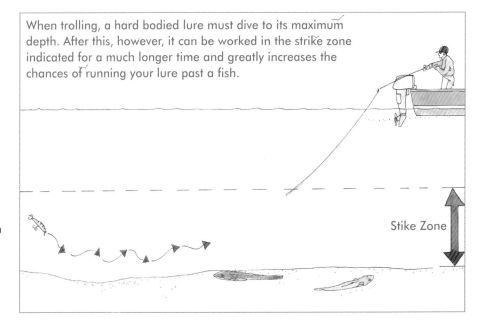

When trolling, a hard bodied lure must dive to its maximum depth. After this, however, it can be worked in the strike zone indicated for a much longer time and greatly increases the chances of running your lure past a fish.

Stike Zone

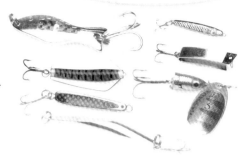

bass and other native species there has been an explosion of options, with lure makers locally turning out different lures by the handful. The StumpJumper range is one of the best trolling lure options here and has the added advantage of interchangeable bibs to vary running depth and action. Other excellent options are from Deception, AC, Oar-Gee and Custom Crafted.

Spoons, slices & wobblers

Spoons, slices and wobblers have been catching fish for centuries and will continue to do so. Spoons and slices are made from metal and cast and sink like rockets, making them easy to fish with in open water situations, but in tight spots they are not preferred. To use a wobbler simply cast it out and let it sink to the desired depth then retrieve at a constant rate to get it into a darting rhythm. Lasers are a bit different as

fish species that will eat a trolled or cast minnow or diving plug. The Classic Barra, the RMG Scorpion and Nilsmaster Invincible are all super lures to cast and troll to all sorts of northern species including barramundi.

For Murray cod, golden perch,

they have a flat profile and must be cranked in a lot faster to get some action into them.

Lasers are great for casting in salt water to salmon, kingfish and tailor, you can also use smaller Lasers in fresh water to jig trout and redfin from a boat. Australia's own Wonder Wobbler has probably caught more varieties and numbers of fish than any other! In fresh water there is no lure more effective for trolling up a trout than the Tassie Devil and the Super Duper is a great variation for trout, redfin and even golden perch. The Pegron Tiger Minnow works well on anything from trout to flathead. Finally, in the surf there's nothing better than the Tailor Ticer or Super Champ.

Surface poppers and paddlers

It's really exciting when a fish hits a surface lure, whether it's a giant trevally up north, a salmon or tailor down south or a bass or saratoga in fresh water, it's all the same—pure adrenaline!

In fresh water you need to pause plenty between each pop or fizz of the lure in the retrieve and you'll find that in a majority of cases the fish will inhale the lure when it's simply sitting on the water inactively! Classic freshwater surface poppers

HINT BOX

Lure Retrieve Speed

Some anglers say that retrieving your lure slower is better and others say that you should do so as quickly as possible. Lures that need to be retrieved quickly are usually sleek and rely on colour or flash to attract a fish's attention. Fish want to catch these lures before they can get away. These are most frequently used in the sea where fast fish hunt their prey with speed.

Fast and flashy

Slower lures are usually used for fish that are ambush feeders, fish that hide in the sand like flathead or amongst snags like barramundi or Murray cod. The fish has to make a decision whether it should leave its hiding place to get the meal, so having the lure in its vision for as long as possible increases the chance of a hook-up. The amount of action—such as wobble, sway or vibration—that a lure produces depends on its shape, and generally the more action that it produces the slower that it can be retrieved. The best slow lures produce a great fish-attracting action at extremely slow speeds. This often entices ambush-feeding fish out of the hiding places by having the lure staying in the fish's zone long enough to entice or annoy it into attacking. Remember that there are lures that work their best in the whole range from extremely fast to almost a dead stop. You should always watch your lure to ensure that it is working at the most appropriate and attractive speed.

Moderate speeds

Slow right down

include the Arbogast Hula Popper, Rapala Skitter Pop and the Arbogast Jitterbug. In salt water the Cotton Cordell Pencil Popper is a classic that brings even deep running fish to the surface to see what the commotion is all about.

Paddlers require a little different approach to poppers and it's usually best to continually slow retrieve them so they get their paddling motion going. Occasional pauses will work and enhance the trip back to the rod tip. The Arbogast Jitterbug is an all-time favourite paddler for many anglers while the Australian Flutterbug and the Halco Night Walker are both great home-grown options.

Spinners

Classic spinners are a standard lure for fresh water and are great for trout in rivers. They are best used by casting and retrieving and the Celta, Mepps and Insect brands are all very popular. The classic Hogback Spinner has proven very successful on native fish and redfin.

Spinnerblades

The use of spinnerblades is becoming more widespread as more and more anglers get used to them and gain confidence in their fish catching abilities. They are very effective on

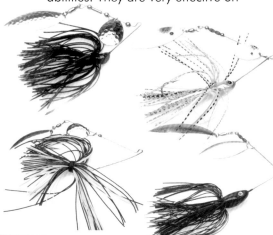

Australian bass, golden perch and Murray cod but also work well on barramundi, trout (using mini sizes), redfin and many other species.

They are primarily a casting lure that is retrieved slowly with a constant retrieve and a rolling wrist action. Anglers have also found that they catch fish on the troll as well and are particularly effective on trolling up Murray cod. They are not all that useful in saltwater fishing situations.

Bibless minnows

Bibless minnows have been around for a while, but it took the introduction of the advanced Jackall and Daiwa models to really capture the imagination of anglers in Australia. Bibless minnow sink fast and have a flat faced nose cut that causes then to have a super tight shake as they are retrieved through the water. Add masses of tiny ball bearings inside a hollow chamber and you have lure that will

interest the dead on a dull day. In the smaller and mid-sized range they are extremely effective on everything from trout, bass, golden perch, flathead and barramundi.

The larger sizes are popular up north in saltwater trolling situations on fish like Spanish mackerel, cobia, tuna and other pelagic species.

Soft plastics

Soft plastic lures have become very popular over the past few years. Their lifelike shapes and movement through the water makes them highly attractive to many fish.

HINT BOX

FRESHWATER

Bass, Australian (*Macquaria novemaculeata*)
Arbogast Jitterbug, Mann's 5+, Rapala Fat Rap FR5, Storm Wiggle Wart, Yo-Zuri Slavko Bug, Heddon Tiny Torpedo, Deception Nipper, Tilsan Bass, 7 gram spinnerbaits, Rebel Crawdad.

Murray cod (*Maccullochella peelii*)
Newell Kadaitcha, Magnum Hellbender, Custom Crafted Hammerhead, Mann's 30+, T50 Flatfish, Predatek 80 mm Boomerang Deep, 42 gram spinnerbait, StumpJumper 1 Deep, Oar-Gee Plow Deep 75, RMG Poltergeist.

Perch, Golden (*Macquaria ambigua*)
Predatek 65 mm Boomerang Deep, Rapala Fat Rap FR7, Storm Hot'N Tot large, Arbogast Mud Bug 1/2oz, Mann's 15+, Eddy Lures Dam Buster, Majik Lures Mulgar, Deception Cherax, Custom Crafted Small Hammerhead, 14 gram spinnerbait.

Perch, Redfin (*Perca fluviatilis*)
Hirst's Harasser Baltic, Rapala Fat Rap 5, Storm Hot'N Tot, No 3 Mepps or Blue Fox, Nilsmaster jig, 4 gram spinnerbait, Ashley Probe, Deception Nipper, Kokoda Yabby, Oar-Gee Lil Ripper.

Trout, Brown (*Salmo trutta*)
Rapala Countdown CD5, Mepps or Blue Fox #2, X4 Flatfish, Rebel Crawfish, Rapala Husky Jerk 6, McGrath Minnow, Tillins Cobra, Pegron Minnow, Worden's Rooster Tail, Tasmanian Devil 13 gram.

Trout, Rainbow (*Oncorhynchus mykiss*)
Size 3 Blue Fox spinner, small Tasmanian Devil, Rapala Countdown CD5, X4 Flatfish, Tilsan Minnow, Halco Laser Pro 45, Rapala Countdown CD3, Tillins Cobra, Pegron Minnow, Worden's Rooster tail.

SALTWATER

Barracouta (*Thyrsites atun*)
Halco Streaker 20 grams, Fishfighter Toby 10 grams, Halco Wobbler 10 grams, Halco Twisty 20 grams, Wonder Spoon 14 grams, Wonder Tubular 28 grams, Halco Hexagon Sparkler 10 grams, Rapala Countdown CD9, RMG Scorpion 68 STD, Bomber Long A Minnow, Pegron Minnow.

Barramundi (*Lates calcarifer*)
Nilsmaster Spearhead, DK Scale Raza 20+, Mann's Boof

Bait, Tilsan Barra, Nilsmaster Invincible series, Cotton Cordell Rattlin' Spot, Rapala Shad Rap, Classic Barra, RMG Scorpion 125, Lively Lures Arafura Barra.

Bream, Yellowfin (*Acanthopagrus australis*)
Oar-Gee Lil Ripper, Halco Laser Pro 45, Deception Palaemon, Taylor Made Nippy Nymph, Attack Lure, RMG Sneaky Bream Suspending, Mirashad Fry, RMG Scorpion 52, Yo-Zuri Slavko Bug, Custom Crafted Shallow Extractor.

Fingermark (*Lutjanus johnii*)
Predatek Boomerang 65 Deep, Rapala Countdown CD9, Halco Laser Pro 100 DD, Storm Deep Thunderstick, DK Scale Raza 20+, Mann's Boof Bait 12+, Custom Crafted Lumo Diver, Predatek Jindivik, Nilsmaster Jumbo DD, C Lures Jack Snack Deep.

Flathead, Bar-tail (*Platycephalus endrachtensis*)
Mann's Stretch 5+, RMG Scorpion 68, Rapala Jointed Shad Rap, Fat Rap 7, Kokoda Dinkum Yabby, Rebel Crawdad, Majik Lures Mulgar, Team Daiwa Hyper Minnow, Storm Deep Thunder Stick, Luhr Jensen Power Minnow.

Flounder (*Pseudorhombus sp*)
Halco Laser Pro 45, Mann's Stretch 5+, RMG Scorpion 52, Rapala Jointed Shad Rap 4, Yo-Zuri Aile Killifish, Rebel Crawdad, Oar-Gee Lil Ripper, Taylor Made Nippy Nymph, Predatek MinMin Deep, Mac's Micro Mauler.

Kingfish, Yellowtail (*Seriola lalandi*)
Kokoda Raptor 40 gram, Hawk Pilchard 90 gram, Halco Wobbler 30 gram, Kokoda Vector 50 gram, Wonder Pilchard 45 gram, Legend Murray Cod Spinnerbait, Halco Crazy Deep 150 DD, Rapala Magnum CD14, Halco Twisty 30 gram, Mann's Heavy Duty Stretch 25.

Mackerel, Spanish (*Scomberomorus commerson*)
Halco Laser Pro 160 DD, Rapala Magnum CD14, Halco 125 STD, Nilsmaster Invincible 15, Halco Giant Trembler, Rapala Magnum CD18, Halco Laser Pro 160 STD, Bomber Long A Magnum, Storm Saltwater Thunderstick.

Mulloway (*Argyrosomus japonicus*)
Killalure Jewie 150, Bill's Bugs Jew Lure 126, Predatek Viper 150, Mann's 12+ Boof Bait, Illusion Lures Wedgetail Deep 12, Illusion Lures Jester, Majik Lures Mulgar 10+, Mudeye Lures Nomad, Larrikin Lures LK 160, RMG Scorpion 125 DD.

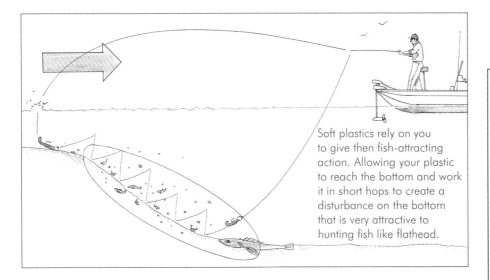

Soft plastics rely on you to give then fish-attracting action. Allowing your plastic to reach the bottom and work it in short hops to create a disturbance on the bottom that is very attractive to hunting fish like flathead.

fact Box

RIGGING JIG HEADS

1. Begin by measuring the tail alongside the jig head and noting exactly where the bend of the hook comes to.

2. Turn the tail upside down and carefully push the hook point into the very centre of the front or nose of the plastic.

3. Feed the plastic tail onto and around the hook bend, keeping the shank of the hook in the centre of the soft plastic.

4. Bring the hook point out at the spot measured in Step 1 and as close to the centreline of the plastic as possible. Add a drop of super glue if so desired.

5. Snug the nose of the plastic hard up against the back of the jig head and check that the tail is straight and properly centred.

As their name suggests, these lures are made from a variety of soft plastics and resins. Modern moulding techniques allow the creation of accurate copies of worms, shrimps, yabbies, prawns and baitfish. Some of these are irresistible to predatory fish on the hunt for food. And, being soft, the fish are often fooled by the lifelike 'feel' of the lures and will attack them repeatedly until they hook up.

The important point is to always use a lure that matches what the target fish like to eat. Bream are attracted to small lures, flathead to larger ones and even larger ones are used on mulloway. Each species of fish needs a little thought when the lure is being selected. This 'action' is partly provided by the shape of the lure, partly by the weight of the jig head and partly by the angler using both the retrieve of the reel and rod tip movement.

The most popular way to rig soft plastics is with a jig head, where the soft plastic is threaded onto the jig head hook. Jig head presentations are by far the most popular, as they are easy to rig and work on a wide variety of fish species. Other methods of rigging include Texas and Carolina rigging, drop shot and wacky rigs—each of these works best in some specific applications. Texas and Carolina work well in lakes on cod and perch, drop shotting is a handy method for trout and is very effective on bream, and wacky rigging is a method to use when you need to just suspend a soft plastic and drift it slowly.

Many anglers now use gelspun or super lines as a matter of course when fishing with soft plastics, this allows the slightest bite or take to be registered back up the line to the angler.

Salmon, Australian (Arripis sp)
Lively Lures Kingfisher Super Blooper, Rapala Skitter Pop 12, Kokoda Roger 10, Halco Wobbler 30 gram, Halco Twisty 30 gram, Rapala Magnum Mag-11, RMG Scorpion, Storm Suspending Thunderstick, Mauler Shallow Runner, Mann's Stretch 1 Minus.

Salmon, Threadfin (Polydactylus sheridani)
Halco Twisty 20 gram, Halco Hex Sparkler 20 gram, Fishfighter Toby 14 gram, Wonder Enticer 28 gram, Halco Wobbler 20 gram, Tilsan Barra, DK Lures Snag Master 6, Predatek Jindivik, RMG Scorpion 68 DD, Bomber Long A Minnow.

Snapper (Pagrus auratus)
Kokoda Raptor 40 grams, Kokoda Vector 30 grams, Rio's Live Chrome 20 grams, Intruder Ko-Jack, Halco Wobbler 30 grams, Rapala Magnum CD9, RMG Scorpion 68 DD, Rattlin' Rapala RNR7, River 2 Sea Diver Vib 65, Rapala Sliver 13.

Tailor (Pomatomus saltatrix)
Kingfisher Mini Turbo, Killalure K9 Popper, Lively Lures Kingfisher Super Blooper, Mustang Lures Bo-Bo, Cotton Cordell Pencil Popper, Halco Wobbler 30 gram, Halco Twisty 30 gram, Fishfighter Toby 14 gram, Wonder Pilchard 15 gram, Lively Lures Blue Pilly.

Trevally (Family Carangidae)
Mal Florence's Master Popper, Kingfisher Mini Turbo, Ambush Lures Ranger 90, Lively Lures Kingfisher Barra, Halco Wobbler 30 gram, Halco Twisty 30 gram, Fishfighter Toby 20 gram, Wonder Pilchard 15 gram, Halco Sparkler 40 gram, Rapala Magnum CD11.

Trout, Coral (Plectropomus leopardus)
Rapala Magnum CD11, Halco Laser Pro 125 DD, Rapala Magnum CD14, Halco 150 XDD Crazy Deep, Nilsmaster Invincible 15, Nomad 120, Bomber Long A Magnum, Storm Saltwater Thunderstick, Predatek Viper 150, Yo-Zuri Hydro Squirt.

Tuna (Thunnus sp)
Rapala Countdown CD14, Halco Laser Pro 160 DD, Halco Trembler 110, Rapala Countdown CD18, Yo-Zuri Hydro Magnum, Storm Deep Thunderstick, Hawk Pilchard 30 gram, Halco Laser Pro 160 STD, Bomber Long A Magnum, Halco Wobbler 30 gram.Pro 160 STD, Bomber Long A Magnum, Halco Hex Sparkler 60 gram.

fact Box

RIGGING SOFT PLASTICS

A standard **Texas Rig**. The weight may be either left free-running, or pegged in place using a sliver of toothpick or match stick pushed into the line channel of the sinker.

A standard **Carolina Rig**, with a worm hook, swivel, glass or plastic bead and running weight. The distance between the swivel and hook can be easily varied.

The **'wacky rig'** is simple and rather unsophisticated, but can be quite effective. Fish it with a gentle up-and-down jigging motion just clear of the bottom.

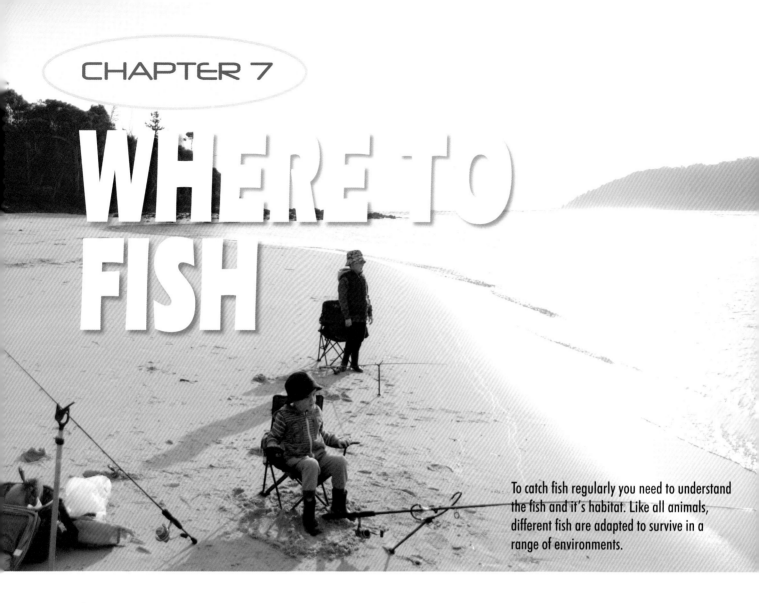

CHAPTER 7

WHERE TO FISH

To catch fish regularly you need to understand the fish and it's habitat. Like all animals, different fish are adapted to survive in a range of environments.

FISH HABITATS

Some fish only live on sand others like rocky, reefy areas. Some live on the surface while others live in mid water or on the bottom.

By fishing with a bait that a particular fish likes to eat and placing the bait where that specie of fish prefers to live, you are most likely to catch the type of fish you are seeking. It's called targeting the fish.

Knowing where particular fish are likely to be living can really help your fishing as you can choose rigs and baits likely to catch the target fish.

The target idea can be a bit more general as well. Fishing a bottom rig baited with a worm or yabby may catch a range of fish that feed over the area. The catch might include whiting, bream and flathead plus a few others depending on where you are fishing. In this case the target

was bottom fish and the bait used was attractive to a wide range of species.

Surface fish are the same. A pilchard or whitebait suspended a metre or so under a float is most likely to be taken by a tailor, salmon, bonito, kingfish or mackerel. Again, the fish are being targeted.

By looking carefully at any piece of water it should be possible to work out what fish are most likely to live there. You can combine your knowledge of the fish with what you catch or what you see being caught by others.

The fish species change as you move around the country, so what you can catch is often determined by where you are fishing. But the fish are still ruled by natural forces and will feed where they have adapted to make their living.

Bream will still be around jetty pylons and rocky banks whether you fish in Melbourne, Sydney or Cairns. They will be slightly different species but bream non-the-less.

The surface fish you encounter will change markedly. In Melbourne it's likely to be a salmon that takes the pilchard under the float, in Sydney it will be a tailor and in Cairns it will be a trevally or mackerel.

All are surface fish and they will all fall for the same technique, it just needs to be used where they are most likely to feed. Learning about where fish live, what they eat and how they feed makes you think about fishing and what you need to do to catch the fish.

It's a great challenge and one of the real keys to successful fishing. Get this bit right and you will catch fish anywhere.

ESTUARY FISHING

The word 'estuary' basically describes the stretch of a coastal river or lake between its mouth and the upper tidal or brackish water limit. An estuary may also be a bay, a lake, a mangrove creek, a harbour, an inlet or a saltwater lagoon.

Estuaries in all their forms carry a huge range of fish in a very diversified spread of habitats, many of which are easily accessible. They are our most popular fishing areas.

Locating fish species

Learning which fish live where is part of the fun of fishing.

Some fish like **bream** are very flexible in their habitat choice and may turn up anywhere. They also eat just about anything so they will take a very wide range of baits.

Mangrove jacks tend to dwell in the matted roots and snags of the mangrove trees that line tropical creeks.

Mulloway like underwater structures such as reef edges, deep holes, pylons and steep drop-offs.

Barramundi patrol the edges of snags and tidal current lines where smaller creeks join the main stream.

King George whiting like isolated patches of sand within extensive weedbeds, while the **east coast sand whiting** prefers sandbanks where they hunt yabbies, worms and small shrimps.

Snapper tend to seek out reefs, wrecks and deeper areas of broken bottom, particularly if lots of shellfish or crabs live in the same area.

Flathead like the edges of channels and holes, although they have a tendency to turn up wherever there is a patch of sand or nearby cover of ribbon weed.

Mullet and **luderick** (blackfish), being herbivorous tend to feed around weedbeds and pylons.

Pylons and other man-made structures are attractive to a wide range of fish, with fish like **leatherjackets** and **luderick** feeding on the pylons and many others like **yellowtail**, **mullet** and **tommy ruff** using the pylons as a holding area.

By fishing an estuary regularly you will soon learn the type of fish that inhabit the various parts of it and you can then choose an area with the type of habitat preferred by your target fish.

When to fish

Fish use time and tide to both hunt and gain access to their preferred feeding areas. Some fish use the low light of dawn and dusk to stage their feeding sprees. Others use the cover

PRIME FLATHEAD LIES

These two illustrations show the sorts of places where flathead will typically tend to position themselves in order to ambush a meal on both the run-out (ebb) and incoming (flood) tides in the lower reaches of an imaginary estuary system. Note that on both tides, flathead will lie facing into the flow (this is something worth thinking carefully about, especially in back-eddies or counter-flows). These hunters will also make use of current breaks, edges and drop offs, both for concealment and to concentrate their prey into narrower 'killing fields'. Always look for the choke points and intersections that will restrict fishy traffic flow!

INCOMING TIDE

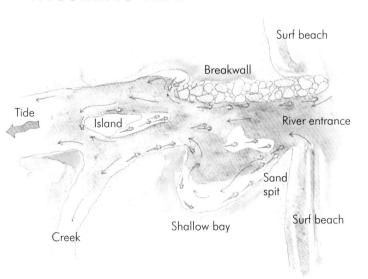

RUN-OUT TIDE

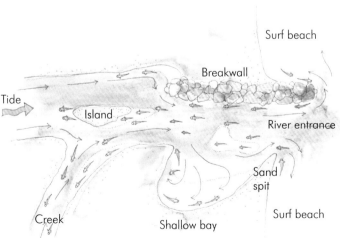

of darkness to gain access to shallow waters where they feed during the night.

The behaviour of many species is strongly linked to the tides and they rely on certain phases of the tidal cycle to bring them food or to allow them access to food-rich areas. Fish in this category include mulloway, whiting, flathead, mangrove jack, barramundi, threadfin salmon and bream.

As the tide falls, baitfish, prawns and other morsels are forced to leave the shelter of mangroves or sandbanks and return to the channels, where predators are sure to be waiting. Estuary flathead in particular, make good use of falling tides to force prey towards their concealed location or 'lie'.

Tides can also be important to fish like whiting, bream, luderick and the many other forage species. A rising tide will give them access to feeding areas like yabby banks, cockle beds and weed covered shorelines.

Tackle

The secret with estuary tackle is to fish as light as possible while still being able to handle the fish hooked. Local fishing conditions will generally dictate the most popular style of rod and reel for a particular area. Hooks should suit the bait size and presentation should always strive for a natural approach with light sinkers suited to the gear and conditions.

Baits

Anglers fishing in the estuary have a wide choice of baits available. Most of these are covered in the sections on baits and species.

The main rule is to fish with baits the target fish like to eat. Baits should always be of top quality and if you have the time you can have a lot of fun just gathering the bait. Some baits like bread and dough come straight from home and others like prawns, pilchards and whitebait can

Salmon are popular in the surf.

did you know ...

FISHING CLUBS

Fishing clubs offer a place for anglers to share a common interest, exchange ideas, learn about their sport, engage in competition and generally add to their enjoyment of the sport. Fishing clubs are good places for young anglers to get information and experience to improve their fishing.

As a rule, young anglers are most welcome at fishing clubs. Some clubs put on regular outings for juniors and junior trophies are awarded in most fishing competitions. In some clubs you may meet people who are willing to take you fishing or just meet other young anglers you can team with to enjoy some extra fishing.

Your local bait and tackle shop can usually tell you where the nearest fishing club is located and the contact number of the president or secretary.

HINT BOX

Beachworm baits

Use pieces of worm long enough to cover the shank of the hook. Leave a small end piece free and make sure that the point of the hook is exposed. Because this worm is tough and elastic, a fish such as a small whiting may not be hooked unless the hook point is left clear.

When baiting up for large fish such as mulloway, the worm should be put on the hook in a series of loops. All these pieces will move especially if attacked by pickers and the general appearance is of a good, bulky bait which mulloway find irresistible.

be obtained at the local tackle shop.

The real secret, no matter what bait you use, is to present it in a way that fish expect to find it. As an example, prawns in the ocean swim straight and flat, the only curled up ones are on anglers hooks. The fish learn this quickly. So you should put a prawn on a hook so it looks like it is alive.

In many cases there is also no substitute for a live bait. A struggling live bait sends out panic signals which some fish just cannot resist. The same bait presented dead may simply be ignored. Prawns are a good example, a live kicking, clicking prawn will usually be vigorously attacked by any fish in the area, a dead prawn may just sit there until a hungry fish comes along.

Lures

Although this topic is covered under the section on lures, fishing with lures in estuaries is both great fun and does catch a lot of fish.

Lure fishing takes a bit of time to learn the basics, but it also teaches you a lot about the fish, how they feed and where they live. An amazing number of fish will take a lure, and the hunting style and active participation makes lure fishing one of the best things available in estuary fishing.

WHARVES AND JETTIES

Right around Australia, wharves, jetties and piers rate as one of the most popular fishing platforms available. For most anglers, their fishing lives started on a pier, wharf or jetty somewhere.

The reason why these structures are so popular is easy to understand. They provide access for anglers, a comfortable, safe environment and are often located in the centre

Fishing on jetties is often a great way to meet and to learn from other anglers.

of town or are connected by public transport.

They also attract and hold a lot of fish. A pier or wharf is a natural haven for fish. Some fish are attracted by the marine life growing on the pylons, baitfish use the jetty as a protected holding area and bigger fish are attracted to the baitfish.

Anglers themselves often help attract fish to such areas by using berley, which encourages fish to congregate in the area.

Where to fish

One problem when fishing a jetty is to decide just where to fish. For those new to the sport, the quickest way to learn is to watch where everyone else is fishing. If the fish are biting you may see them being landed. Without

crowding anyone else, fish close to the area and you should also catch the fish.

Also, watch carefully how the successful anglers are rigged, what bait they use and how they present it to the fish. By copying what they are doing you will increase your chances.

As a general rule, most jetties fish best at the deeper end. Deeper water offers a wider range of fish habitats and fish types. Shallow water is more likely to produce fish like whiting, garfish, mullet, flathead, leatherjackets and other forage feeders, but these fish may also bite in the deeper water.

When to Fish

The best time to fish from wharves and jetties is usually early in the

morning through to about 10 a.m. and then again in the afternoon from about 3 p.m. through to early evening. The tide can also be important. As a rule, most jetties fish best at the change of tide when the tidal movement slows, then stops and then runs back in the opposite direction.

If fishing shallow water, the rising tide is usually best as feeding fish will follow the rising water to gain access to food. In areas where the jetty reaches the edge of a deep channel, the channel area will fish best at low tide as fish are forced out of the shallows and into the deeper water.

Some jetties fish better at night when the fish are attracted by the bright lights illuminating the area.

Tackle

Because there are lots of different fish available from jetties a wide range of gear can be used, it depends a lot on what you want to catch, and what fish are caught in the area.

Most people start with a handline or light rod and reel. Handlines are convenient as they catch plenty of fish and are very cheap to purchase.

Rods and reels

The best rod and reel to start with is a light, single handed rod about 1.5 to 2 metres long fitted with either a small threadline or sidecast reel. If you need to cast any distance then a longer rod would be a good choice. The secret here is to make sure the casting rod is light enough for you to use comfortably. Big, heavy rods only work well in the hands of big, heavy people so keep the weight down and you'll have more fun.

For fish like luderick, garfish, mullet and tommy ruff a long whippy rod works best as it allows for the easy working of the float rigs often used to catch these fish.

Technique

How you rig your line and what bait you use will determine what type of fish you catch.

---

did you know ...

FISHING AROUND BRIDGES

Bridges offer lots of fishing opportunities for anglers. Most of the fishing needs a boat, but there are some bridges where angling is allowed.

When fishing from a bridge always fish in line with the pylons, that way your gear cannot interfere with or injure anyone passing beneath in a boat. Bridge pylons can sometimes be accessed and make a great platform for anglers if they have the right shape.

As bridges often straddle rivers and estuaries they can provide excellent spots for fish to rest and feed. They hold

lots of baitfish, which also attracts big fish.

When fishing around bridges always watch the tides, they can run fast in many places. So choose times when tidal flows are least, the change of the tide or neap tides.

Bridges are almost always lit at night and these bright lights also attract hunting fish looking for bait. So a night fish around a bridge is often worthwhile.

Learn about the bridges in your area as they nearly always hold a few good fish.

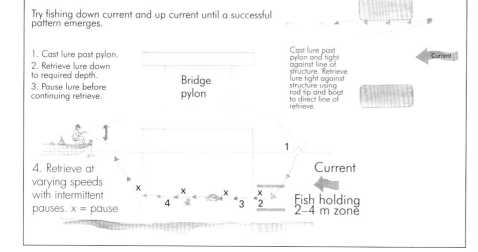

Try fishing down current and up current until a successful pattern emerges.

1. Cast lure past pylon.
2. Retrieve lure down to required depth.
3. Pause lure before continuing retrieve.

Bridge pylon

Cast lure past pylon and tight against line of structure. Retrieve lure tight against structure using rod tip and boat to direct line of retrieve.

Current

4. Retrieve at varying speeds with intermittent pauses. x = pause

Current

Fish holding 2–4 m zone

Despite the tremendous number of different fish available from wharves and jetties you really only need to know about six rigs to cover almost all of the fish available.

This is because the rigs can be adapted to suit the fish in each area and some species like whiting, bream, leatherjacket, mullet and garfish can be found right around the country.

Best baits

The best baits for wharf and jetty fishing include prawns, worms, bread, dough, pilchards, whitebait, shellfish, maggots and small live fish. Bait selection is governed by the type of fish you want to catch and what is available at the location being fished.

Prawns are a great stand-by as nearly everything eats them. For small fish you can peel the prawn and use it one segment at a time and for bigger

HINT BOX

Don't scare the fish

Fish of all sizes are essentially food for other fish, birds of prey or marine mammals. Because just about every fish can be attacked and eaten by something, they have developed acute defence mechanisms to protect themselves.

Most successful anglers try to avoid doing things that scare fish. While sounds made in air do not transmit into water, sounds made in the water travel a lot further in water than in the air.

Any loud sound made on the hull of a boat like a dropped anchor, tackle box or heavy object will alarm the fish in the surrounding water.

Fish which feed by sight can be spooked easily by an angler walking along a bank and getting too close to the fish. Fish like trout, bass, flathead, whiting and mullet can be spooked by a careless approach to their feeding area. Anything you do that might scare the fish needs consideration. Good anglers don't scare fish, they catch them.

FISH FACT

SEAHORSE

The seahorse gets its name because its head, neck and torso looks like those of a horse. It swims upright in the water swaying from side to side.

The seahorse has a versatile tail that it uses to hold itself in among seagrass and rocks, which it uses for protection and to attack its unsuspecting prey. It waits motionless until a small fish or shrimp swims innocently by and then eats it.

One of the oddest things about the seahorse is that the father gives birth to the young. The female seahorse deposits the eggs in the male's brood pouch then goes off on her happy way. When the young hatch they emerge from the fathers body and swim off on their own.

There are about fifty different seahorses world wide, ranging in size from about 25 mm to 380 mm high and they are a wide variety of colours.

fish you can use a whole prawn. Worms are also very good bait but tend to be a bit expensive.

Bread and dough can be used and pilchards and whitebait are very good for fish that like to eat other fish.

Berley

Berley is very important when fishing from jetties. This is because you are

normally fishing from a fixed position and berley attracts and holds the fish to that location. By concentrating the fish near the wharf, the chances of a good catch are maximised.

Accessories

There are lots of bits and pieces you can carry for jetty fishing but probably the most important is a bucket with a rope attached for obtaining water and for keeping bait or small fish alive. Always carry something to keep your fish in, either a keeper net, bucket, ice box or a bag of some kind.

Do the right thing

Don't forget to leave the jetty clean and tidy when you finish fishing. Don't leave any bait or fish on the wharf or leave any litter lying around. Most importantly, don't throw any plastic bags or wrappers in the water. These damage the fish, smother the bottom life and can cripple power boats by blocking their cooling water intakes.

If everyone does the right thing it helps the environment and helps give anglers a good name.

BEACH FISHING

Light tackle beach fishing is very productive and lots of fun. There are plenty of beaches to fish and the same technique works right around the coast.

Beach tackle

The ideal rod is about 3.2 to 3.5 m long with a medium to fast taper. Light weight is essential but the rod still needs a bit of spine for handling the big tailor and salmon sometimes found in late autumn and early winter. The rod also needs the good casting attributes of medium to fast taper rods. These rods work best with light line between 4 and 8 kilograms.

One important factor is the choice of reel. Narrow spool 500, 550 or 600 size Alvey sidecasts are popular as are medium sized threadlines.

Sinker weights used are generally

Australia's big, open beaches provide lots of scope for anglers.

between 30 and 60 g depending on the conditions. The calmer and clearer the conditions the lighter the lead used. Ball sinkers suit this kind of fishing very well and allow good casting and the presentation of moving baits.

Beach baits

Select a hook to suit the bait rather than the fish being chased. Bait selection as in almost every type of fishing is critical.

The main bait for daylight fishing is beachworms. Preserved worms are a poor second to live ones, but are passable. When fishing with beachworms Long Shank hooks of either No. 2 or No. 4 size is used.

Keep an eye open for any pipis that happen to get washed down the beach while fishing. The pipi is a tough bait and can hang together better than worms if pickers are proving a problem. The pipis are used mostly on bream but other fish also find them attractive. Pipi and fish flesh baits are fished on No. 2 Suicide, sliced shank hooks. These are mostly a bream hook and their light gauge steel does not seem to put shy fish off the bite.

Fish flesh like tuna, bonito or slimy mackerel cut into strips makes excellent bait for bream, tailor and flathead. Pilchards, both whole and in sections are also very good.

When fishing for tailor or salmon, whitebait or blue pilchards are the best baits.

Tailor gangs are made up on 3/0 or 4/0 Limerick hooks.

PIPIS

Pipis are shellfish that are frequently used for bait when fishing in estuaries and from beaches. They are found near the waterline of surf beaches at low tide. The smooth, rounded shells of pipis can be located with the toes by shuffling or twisting in the sand near the water's edge with bare feet. They are normally close to the surface and are easily gathered.

Finding fish

Many anglers talk about 'reading' a beach. The real truth is that the fish are where you find them. You can find two holes that look identical and one will be barren and the other full of fish. The reason is not clear but it could relate to the availability of food and shelter. Therefore the best way is to look for certain features and try these first.

When looking at a beach and analysing the likely spots, always look for places where there is a mix of white water, green water and sloping sandbanks.

Many fish will be found in the gutter between the outer break and the beach break. While, a lot of others are right at your feet just behind the beach break. This applies particularly to whiting.

Whiting are regularly found in big numbers along the edge of sandbanks that drop into deeper water. If whiting fishing, look especially for mounds or shoulders in the middle of flat beach sections. These mounds often hold a lot of worms and pipis and consequently, feeding whiting.

Look for open-ended gutters that have deep water between the shore and the outer bank. A reasonable surf break of anything up to about 1.5 m is usually quite good. Around 1 m is ideal. Gutters that empty to seaward do tend to give the fish good access to the feeding areas.

Tailor like the big gutters and usually prowl the mid water area between the outer bank and the shore. The best tailor gutters have an opening to seaward at each end. Big holes on the beach will also hold tailor.

One certain way of finding fish is not to stay in one spot for too long. If the fish don't bite within fifteen minutes, they are probably not there. If you don't get bites after a reasonable time move to the next formation. Even a move to the other end of the gutter can make the difference.

Tides play a part, with rising tides tending to carry more fish towards the beach. If the low tide is right on dawn then good fishing should be expected through the morning. Falling tides can also cause the seas to break in important feeding areas so don't write off a falling tide. Often it depends on the beach being fished.

Conditions that don't produce fish

There are conditions that do not produce fish on beaches. Massive, boisterous or churning surf is not popular with the fish, nor is a dead flat, crystal clear sea conducive to good fishing.

The exception to this is tailor and salmon, which often push baitfish against the shoreline during winter westerlies.

Strong longshore drift where you have to jog along to stay with your rig is usually not good for angling. The fish may be there, but they usually don't bite.

There is nothing like a kids smile when he catches a fish.

Each beach is different and takes a little time and patience to master. If four-wheel drive access is available, they certainly help to cover the spots, but plenty of people get by on foot. The important thing is to take the trouble to learn, study and most importantly to try your beach.

Tactics

The one point of technique that is important while fishing the surf is to keep the bait moving. Casting out and having the bait anchored in one spot or setting the rod in a sand spike is a sure way to catch nothing. The bait should be cast out and allowed to settle. If no bites are forthcoming retrieve 3 m of line and wait another half a minute. Continue the process until the rig is close to the inshore break. This system allows you to cover all the available fishing water. On whiting, a very slow but continuous retrieve is particularly effective.

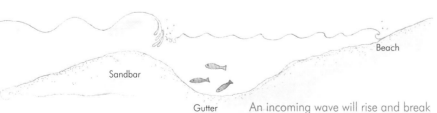

Cross section of a beach gutter

Sandbar

Gutter

Beach

An incoming wave will rise and break on the sandbar where the water shallows. The force of the wave is lost so the water looks to be calm between the sandbar and the shore. But as the water pushes towards the shore, it rises again where it comes out of the gutter and into the higher level of sand.

If your reel falls into the sand

Having a fishing reel fall into the sand is a common problem that all beach fishermen run into at some stage. A sand-covered reel can bring an abrupt end to a hot fishing session, or worse prolonged use could damage the reel's internal engineering.

For this reason, the most basic reel designs are often the most popular with beach anglers. Sidecast reels are perfectly suited to beach fishing as they can be rinsed in the surf to clean them of sand, yet remain fully functional.

Should a threadline or overhead reel become the victim and be dropped in the sand, the consequences are often much more serious. A light covering of sand can usually be wiped or blown away without any dire effects, however, if sand has penetrated the internals, a full strip down of the reel and thorough cleaning is in order. Never wash a threadline or overhead reel in saltwater, the long term effects will far exceed the damage done by being dropped in the sand.

For most reels a good wash under the tap, take the spool off and clean it and some oil or spray lubricant on the shaft will have everything running well again.

The great advantage of this fishing style is the direct contact with the lead and any bites that come along are registered. Surf fish feed vigorously and don't muck about with the bait. When a bite is felt just turn the reel handle until the weight of the fish starts to load the rod tip. Lean back and the fish will be hooked.

Light tackle surf gear takes a little skill when playing the fish, particularly big ones. Use the rod as a shock absorber and make sure the drag is set correctly. Once the fish is close to the white water walk slowly backwards and use the wash to bring

the fish up the beach. Do not try and drag a fish against a falling wash. This type of tackle is not capable of bulldozing tactics, so take your time and enjoy the fight.

Beach fishing can really get you in. It is a very relaxing sport, with the roar of the surf keeping conversations to a minimum.

OFFSHORE FISHING

Fishing offshore can be exciting and offers the anglers a chance at some big fish. It also has the challenge of learning about the ocean and the fish, mammals and birds that live in it and on it.

did you know ...

GREAT BARRIER REEF

Australia's Great Barrier Reef is the largest coral reef in the world. It is not really one reef but a chain of coral formations stretching more than 2000 kilometres down the eastern coast of tropical Queensland.

The reef starts up off the coast of New Guinea and runs south down to around Gladstone. It is one of the most complex webs of life on the planet with more than 1000 species of fish plus corals, shellfish, worms, crustaceans, sponges and all manner of interesting organisms.

Having a dive or a snorkel on the Great Barrier Reef is a real learning experience, far more fun and exciting than anything you can see on the TV.

There are several different types of fishing available when you go to sea.

Bottom fishing

Many people go to sea to catch table fish such as snapper, flathead, morwong, coral trout, sweetlips, emperor, tassie trumpeter and many, many more species.

There is a real thrill in lowering a bait over the side, dropping it into the depths and then hooking a fish. The fish can be small or large and it may be one of a dozen or more species.

Bottom fishing can be carried out successfully with either a handline or rod and reel. Handlines need control and the line needs to be carefully laid hand over hand into neat coils on the deck or the bottom of the boat. A rod and reel needs to be worked so the line is kept tight all the time and the line laid neatly on the reel.

The technique for either does not change much. The bait is lowered to the bottom and when a bite is felt the rod or handline is lifted in a quick strike to set the hook. The fish is then played to the surface and either lifted aboard, netted or gaffed depending on the size of the fish.

Sport and game fishing

Sport and game fishing is a fun way to catch fish that provide a challenge either in the way the fish is caught or with light gear that makes for a good fight once the fish is hooked. The average family runabout makes a good platform for light tackle sportfishing. Small boats can also catch quite large fish if used correctly.

Game fishing tends to concentrate on oceanic predators such as marlin, big tuna and sharks. Many of the boats involved are large and well equipped. If you get the chance to go out and experience some game fishing don't miss it, the thrills and spills provide an insight into the greatest fish that swim.

Sport and game fishing uses a very wide range of tackle, so if you are new to this type of fishing you will need to learn how to handle the gear. This takes a little time but not too long. Always ask someone if you need something explained. Don't worry if you make a few mistakes either, that happens to everyone and it is part of learning any sport.

Always be ready to help out on the boat too. Anyone can use a cleaning cloth or scrubbing brush to help tidy the boat when the fishing is over. Skippers always appreciate crewmembers who help with the dirty work.

Balancing offshore tackle

Offshore fishing uses a very wide range of fishing tackle. Much of this tackle is designed for adults and as a result it can be heavy and awkward for young anglers to use. So when starting out, the best advice for young anglers and those who fish with them, is to use tackle that is comfortable and easy for the angler to use.

This may mean that the rod and reel is smaller and lighter than what an adult may use to do the same job. This is not a problem so long as the angler is comfortable. Today quality tackle is also very well engineered and any concessions made with the rod and reel can be compensated for by using a heavier breaking strain line.

Some points should be taken into account when buying gear for offshore angling. Narrow spool reels are easier to handle than wide spool reels. Level wind reels make a lot of sense as the level wind mechanism automatically ensures the line is neatly wound onto the reel.

Rods should be light and bend fairly easily. The butt length should be less than 40 cm, closer to 30 cm is

better. If that means altering a standard production rod that is no problem, your local tackle shop can alter the butt length without any problem.

What strength line you catch your fish on is not really important particularly while learning. Heavy line is a better teacher than light line because you lose less fish on heavy line.

Once you have mastered the art of playing the fish correctly and feel comfortable with the gear, then lighter lines can be used if you want more sport or want to fish specific line classes under fishing club or association rules.

FRESHWATER FISHING

Freshwater fishing is very popular right around Australia with a wide range of fish available, that varies according to where you happen to be fishing. Some of the fish like trout, Murray cod and barramundi are highly prized, others are just fun to catch or good to eat. In a lot of places you can also catch crustaceans such as yabbies and Murray crays.

Freshwater fishing varies tremendously with four main groups of fish being available. These are the Murray Darling group, cold water group, east coast temperate and tropical freshwater.

Snapper are much sought after. When they are on the bite the action can be fast and furious.

Murray Darling Catchment group

The Murray-Darling Catchment drains a huge area of Australia's land mass. There are seven main angling species to be found in this river system that runs through four states.

These fish are Murray cod, golden perch (also know as yellowbelly or callop), silver perch, Macquarie perch and catfish. These fish are all native to the inland rivers. These

did you know ...

CANOES FOR FISHING

Canoes and kayaks make very good fishing platforms in streams, rivers lakes and estuaries. They are fun to use, easy to carry and they help you to catch more fish.

Like any boat they provide mobility and greatly increase the fishing options available. You can paddle along and troll a lure, cast at snags, pump some yabbies or have a drift around. The movement and stability of these craft is different to a normal boat or dinghy but you will get used to them quickly. Canoes and kayaks are fun to paddle, get you mobile, keep you fit and catch more fish. You can't beat that.

When fishing it is essential to wear a life jacket for extra safety.

ABOVE: Many of Australia's dams are stocked with native fish and attract anglers from all over.

LEFT: Worms are one of the best all-round baits in fresh water.

Cold water group

Trout are an introduced fish with rainbow trout coming from North America and brown trout from Europe. They were introduced in the last century by anglers looking to provide a sports fish in our highland streams. Subsequently, brook trout, Atlantic salmon and chinook salmon have all been added to the cold water fishery.

western drainage fish have also been introduced into many dams and water storages with great success. Introduced species such as carp and redfin will also be found in many areas.

The Murray-Darling fish can be fished for with either baits or lures. Bait is generally the most successful with worms, shrimps, yabbies and wood grubs all being productive. Lures work well in dams and on rivers when the water is fairly clear, with Murray cod, yellowbelly and redfin being the main lure takers.

Trout and salmon can only survive in cool to cold water. Once the water temperature rises above 20°C most rainbow trout die. Brown trout can handle slightly warmer temperatures. This need for cool water has restricted their distribution to highland and cold climate areas.

Trout are found in New South Wales, Victoria, Tasmania, South Australia and Western Australia.

Some areas are famous for their trout fishing, like the lakes and rivers of the Snowy Mountains, the Victorian highlands and Central Plateau of Tasmania.

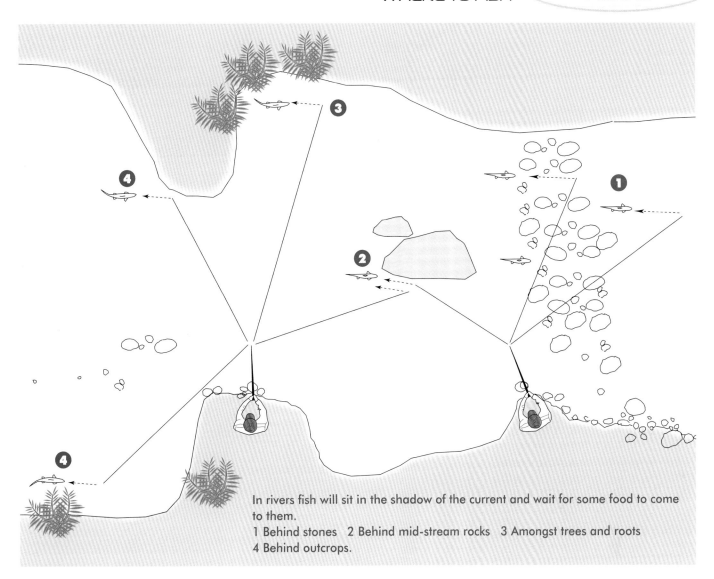

In rivers fish will sit in the shadow of the current and wait for some food to come to them.
1 Behind stones   2 Behind mid-stream rocks   3 Amongst trees and roots
4 Behind outcrops.

Trout can be caught using bait, lures or flies and whole books are available on the subject. For beginners the easiest way to catch a trout is either trolling from a boat in one of the dams or by using a worm or small spinner in a highland stream or lake.

Wherever you fish for them, trout are great fun to catch and their spectacular jumps when hooked adds to the thrill of the game.

East Coast temperate group

The East Coast freshwater fishery starts around Maroochydore and goes all the way around to the Victorian/South Australian border. The main species are Australian bass and estuary perch, plus mullet, catfish and eels. Two

cod species, the Mary River cod and eastern freshwater cod are also found in a few rivers and dams.

Bass and estuary perch are related and hard to tell apart, so we'll treat them as the one fish. Both fish live in the upstream parts of rivers from about where the tidal and saltwater influence stops right up to the pools in the foothills of the mountain ranges.

These fish are aggressive hunters and take both lures and baits keenly. They spend a lot of their time near structure, which they use as a base for attacking fish and insects as they swim or drift past. Snags, fallen trees, overhanging bushes, sheer rock walls and undercut banks are all good places to look for these fish.

Both fish are great lure takers and a cast close to a snag or wherever the fish is hiding will often be rewarded with a crashing strike.

Bass rely on being able to migrate between fresh and saltwater to spawn, Moving downstream in late autumn and upstream in early spring.

Both species have also suffered badly through habitat destruction and bag limits apply to the number you can legally capture. Despite this, there are still plenty of bass about if you take the trouble to learn about their habits. They are a great challenge and real fun to catch.

Mullet, catfish and eels are all caught on bait and are popular in many areas. Carp can also be found in many of our eastern flowing rivers.

Tropical freshwater group

Tropical rivers provide great fishing over nearly half the continent. The main target species are barramundi, saratoga, sooty grunter, jungle perch, catfish, archer fish and a few saltwater fish that readily adapt to the freshwater environment.

The fishing environment varies from the thundering streams of the north Queensland rainforest through to the still billabongs of the Northern Territory flood plains. Like everywhere else, wherever there is clean water there will be fish to catch.

Most of the popular tropical species are all keen lure takers and great sport can be had tossing lures around the rivers and billabongs. These fish will also take baits, with shrimps, prawns, worms, large insects and small fish all being popular.

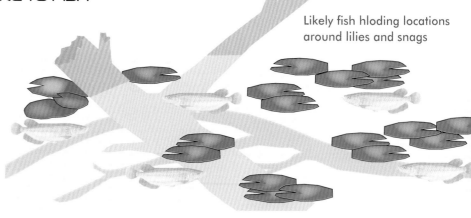
Likely fish hloding locations around lilies and snags

Access can be a problem in some areas, with a boat or canoe being necessary to get to the best fishing. However anglers who are willing to walk will find access points on many of the rivers.

Surprisingly good fishing can be found around many north Queensland towns by anglers who take the time and trouble to learn where the fish are to be found.

FISH FACT

MANTIS SHRIMP

Mantis shrimp are a weird and fierce looking shrimp that lives in estuaries and close offshore waters. Scientifically known as squilla these shrimp look much like a praying mantis insect and they do feed in a similar way.

They make a tube-like burrow in the sand and sit just inside the entrance waiting for a prawn or small fish to pass close enough. When something edible does stray close, they flash out their pronged pincers and seize it. They then drag it down their burrow and devour their lunch.

If you think the squilla reminds you of something then it probably does. The head of the alien monster in the movie Predator is modelled on a squilla. The creator of the movie picked one up at a fish market, looked at it and the idea was born.

So it's not an alien at all, just a scary shrimp you can find in almost every estuary in Australia.

did you know ...

FISH LADDERS

Also called fish staircases, these are a series of small pools graduated in height, and usually connected by a sloping channel. They allow fish to move upstream and downstream at manmade barriers like weirs and dams. Without this movement some fish species would die out as they need to migrate so they can spawn.

Both trout and salmon have the ability to leap great distances up rapids, allowing them to negotiate the ladders with ease. After each leap upwards they rest in the pool until they reach their destination.

Fish ladders for Australian native fish have also been developed to allow our great local river fish to migrate and breed. These fish ladders use larger pools and deeper staircases to provide bypasses at weirs and dams and will hopefully assist these fish to increase in numbers.

A lot of work is currently being done to provide fish ladders particularly in the Murray-Darling and they will become a common sight at most weirs and barrages.

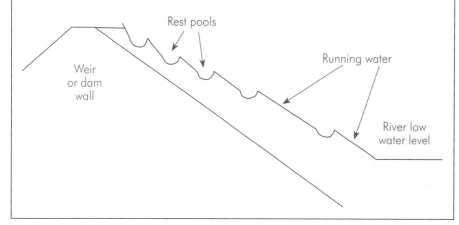
Rest pools
Weir or dam wall
Running water
River low water level

Keys to freshwater fishing

Catching freshwater fish relies on the same principles whether you are on a frosty mountain trout stream or a steamy tropical river. Fish are adapted to use the water movement to bring them food and they use the geography of the stream to provide them with a base for their hunting.

Feeding fish face upstream into the current, this makes it easy for them to breath and it is the direction from which they expect food to be carried on the current. Predatory fish often launch their attacks from cover so they usually hold station near snags, overhanging vegetation, along deep drop-offs or rocky walls and behind large boulders that obstruct the current.

Reading the river, also known as stream craft, is an essential part of the exercise. If you can look at the stream and pick the places where a fish is most likely to be hiding, you will catch more fish.

Finding fish in dams, billabongs and other still water locations can be a bit harder but there are a few

Brown trout are much sought after in fresh water.

basics that hold true. Fish like to hold near cover. Areas around snags, sunken timber, boulder gardens and sheer drop-offs are all very likely spots. Any area that holds a lot of food will also be visited by the predators. Along the edges of weedbeds, lily pads or tree lines

is always worthwhile. Any river or stream that enters a lake will be treated as a source of food by the fish and is a likely place to start looking.

The final trick is to present a bait or lure that the fish like to eat and place it, troll it or work it where they are most likely to be feeding or waiting in ambush. The answer will come as the fish takes the bait or strikes the lure.

HOLIDAY FISHING

Holidays are always fun but they also allow you more time and more options for fishing opportunities than would usually be the case. Holiday fishing allows you to try your skills in new places and catch species of fish not available in your usual fishing spots. Catching different types of fish is one of the genuine thrills of going fishing. It is surprising how many people remember vividly their first trout, mulloway, barramundi or whatever.

Things like catching live baits or prawns can be done the day or night before you go fishing and the bait kept alive for the next day. You can fish a bit later or perhaps use the tide better or you may have access to a hire boat or a friend's boat.

Banks with rocks or trees will usually provide a hunting ground for fish.

Fishing competitions for kids, like this annual event at Rowville Lakes are a fun, learning experience.

Whatever the reasons, holidays usually provide lots of options for anglers to go out and catch some fish.

What sort of fishing you do depends a lot on where you are, what sort of tackle you have and what type of access you have to a boat or canoe.

Having a boat or going out in a boat is always a help as it can open up lots of areas that cannot be fished from the shore. But if you don't have a boat don't worry, plenty of good fish are caught by shore-based anglers, you just have to think a bit more about what you are doing and look for the most likely spots.

What fish?

When you go on holidays, the first thing you need to know is what fish are available in the area and decide which ones you might have access to and be able to catch. You need to put yourself in a position where you have a realistic chance of catching the target fish.

For example, lots of big marlin are caught off Cairns, but it all happens a long way out to sea, you need a big boat and sophisticated fishing tackle. But you could easily catch a barramundi, trevally, mangrove jack,

cod, javelin fish or tarpon in and around Cairns Inlet. This can be done from a small boat, hire boat or even a local jetty.

The answer lies in getting good information about the area. The best information can usually be obtained at the local bait and tackle shop or through reading local fishing guides that show the spots and the fish

available in that region. You can do lots of research just by looking around. If there is a crowd of anglers all fishing together you should be able to see what they are catching. They are usually fishing at that spot for a good reason. The same thing happens out in the boat, many good spots will be marked by other anglers fishing there.

You can develop your fish finding skills too and go looking for what you think are likely spots for the fish you are seeking. This is very satisfying, particularly when you catch the fish you were looking for.

Hire boats

One good way to get out on the water in many places is a hire boat. Usually this means having a parent or older friend come along but hire boats will let you get at the fish that cannot be reached by shore fishing. Hire boats are also handy when visiting freshwater lakes as they can be used to troll lures, which is generally more successful than fishing from the shore.

If you go on holidays in a coastal town you may like to go out to sea on a charter boat. Many towns have

Australian salmon are a great sporting fish no matter what size.

Fly fishing is fun and effective.

Floating objects for dolphin fish

Dolphin fish or mahi mahi have a fascination for anything that floats on the surface of the ocean. They will gather under and around it and sometimes gather in big numbers. Anglers around the world use this trait to attract dolphin fish so they can catch them.

In Malta, the Pacific and Carribean Islands people use rafts made of palm leaves and leave them to drift in the open ocean.. In Mexico and South America it's logs draped with old coarse netting or ropes.

Australia and many other countries use Fish Attracting Devices (FADs). These are buoys anchored to the bottom and set in ocean currents. They quickly attract baitfish and the dolphin fish that feed on them. Having a buoy set in place makes it easy for anglers to find and then catch some hard fighting and good eating dolphin fish.

This beautiful dolphin fish was taken from the yellow buoy in the background.

boats operating that take anglers out fishing. You can get information on charter boat fishing in any area from the local tourist information centre.

Holiday learning

Going holiday fishing is all about fun learning, finding out about new places and learning about new fish. If you holiday in the same place each year you will quickly build up a good knowledge of what can be caught and where and this knowledge will build every time you visit the place.

If you don't catch much don't worry, plenty of good fishermen have the same experience. Holidays offer you the chance of something different and some challenge to learn more about fishing.

Kids love big fish.

CHAPTER 8

FIGHTING & LANDING A FISH

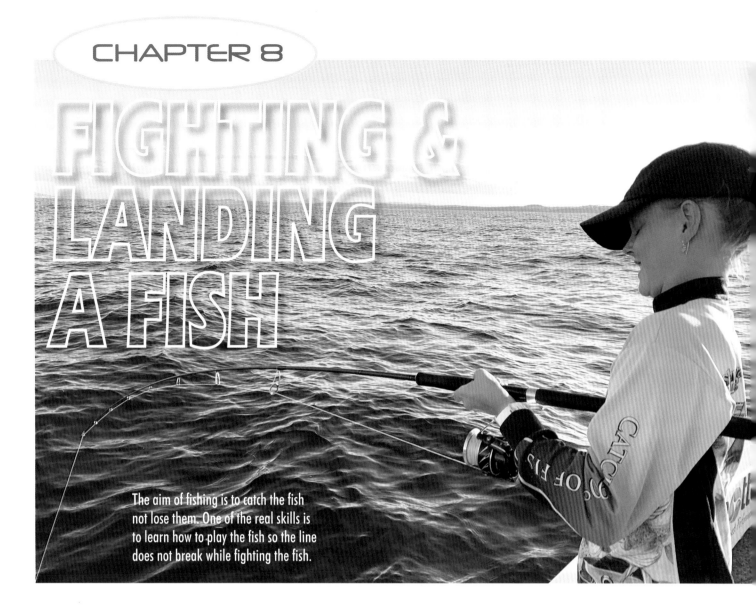

The aim of fishing is to catch the fish not lose them. One of the real skills is to learn how to play the fish so the line does not break while fighting the fish.

To help you play the fish most reels are fitted with a drag. This device allows you to set a controlled amount of tension for the fish to pull against. When the fish pulls harder than the amount of tension set on the reel, the drag will automatically pay out line. This stops the line from breaking.

Pump and wind technique

The way to play a fish is to lean back on the rod and draw the fish towards you and then wind in as you lower your rod, then you take another lean back on the fish, all the time maintaining a bend in the rod. The pump and wind technique is the most effective method of fighting a fish.

This technique should not allow the fish any slack line, some tension must be kept on the fish at all times,

particularly when winding down to recover more line.

Also, remember that reels are not winches, they store line and help play the fish but the angler has to do the work and retrieve the line and the fish.

When fighting a fish with a handline your thumb and forefinger becomes a very sensitive drag mechanism. When the fish pulls hard you can let it run by using your thumb and forefinger to apply pressure to the line. Not too much pressure though, the line has to be able to run out as the fish lunges and surges about.

Netting fish

The last part of landing a fish is usually the most important, getting it out of the water. More fish are lost

at this stage than at any other point in the fight. The vital thing is to take your time and not rush the finish.

There are lots of ways to land a fish. The simplest is to use the rod and reel and lift the fish straight out of the water. This is fine for small fish but remember a fishing line can only lift about a quarter of its breaking strain. So a 3 kg line can only lift a fish of 750 g with any safety.

To improve the odds, most anglers use a landing net. The fish is played out and then netted and safely landed. The main thing to remember with the landing net is to come from beneath the fish and lift, with the whole fish falling into the net. The person with the net holds it in the water and the angler leads the fish to the net.

Do not come from behind the fish

LEFT: The right way to net a fish. The fish is lead towards the net which is already waiting in the water.

BELOW LEFT: The net is driven forward and upwards. This forces the fish into the net head first and envelops the whole fish within the landing net.

BELOW: With the hooks removed the barramundi can be revived and released.

The angler then places their hand, with fingers spread widely, under the balance point of the fish, usually just forward of the middle part of the fish. The fish is then smoothly lifted into the boat or onto the bank.

The fish will stay in this position for a few seconds but not for too long. Once landed place the fish where you can handle it for release or capture.

Tail grip

Large surface fish with rigid tails like trevally, kingfish, mackerel, queenfish and tuna can be easily tail gripped and lifted aboard.

HINT BOX

Aquariums—a place to learn

Many places in Australia have high quality aquariums where you can observe a fascinating variety of marine life.

Visiting an aquarium is great fun not just because of the fish on show, but you can learn about how fish behave in the water. Look where the snapper, trevally or whatever sit in the water column. See how they move or don't move around. Try to learn things from what you see.

Some of the tanks offer great lessons in fish camouflage and how they use their colours.

If you are there at feeding time watch how they feed, which ones are greedy, which ones are shy.

A trip to the aquarium is fun but it is also a learning experience for anyone interested in fish or fishing.

with the net or chase the fish around with it. Just stay calm and cool and let the angler bring the fish back to you and then take the fish correctly.

If you are on your own, you net the fish in exactly the same way except that you lift the rod to bring the fish close enough to net.

When fishing from the shore or beach it is possible to gently slide the fish up the bank. On a beach, quite big fish can be stranded by gently using the surf to surge the fish up the beach. The fish is secured by picking it up when the wave has receded.

In an estuary where you have no surf to wash the fish up, the best option off the shore is still a net. If you don't have one you can still lead the fish into very shallow water and strand it. Once stranded, the fish can be gently swept up the shore by placing your foot (which must have a shoe on) beside the middle of the fish and then sweeping, not kicking, the fish up the shore.

Once stranded, the fish can be

secured by gripping it in the gills. Always be careful landing the fish as many of the fish will be destined for release and you will want them to be in good condition.

Comfort lift

The comfort lift is an old method for gently landing fish and it works on just about all fish except flathead.

The key is to play the fish out and have it swimming on its side.

The comfort lift supports the fish firmly but gently and allows you to bring it aboard.

Once stranded, it is easy to tail grip the fish.

Play the fish to the boat and lift it to the surface. When it is in position it can be gripped firmly by the wrist of the tail and lifted aboard. The fish is then turned upside down by using your spare hand as a cradle.

The fish will be disorientated by being upside down and will generally lay quite still while the hooks are removed. Turn the fish the right way up to release it.

Gaffing

While many big fish are released, some will be kept for the table. In locations like breakwalls and off the rocks, the only way to land a big fish is with a gaff. A gaff is a large barbless hook bound onto an aluminium or fibreglass pole.

When a large fish needs to be captured, the fish is played into position and the gaff is sunk securely into the shoulder or breastplate of the fish. It is then lifted aboard or onto the rocks and the catch is secured.

Tools for releasing fish

Environet

Environets have a smooth inner lining so the fish's protective body slime is not damaged during the landing process. Landing nets with coarse netting and netting knots can damage the fish's protective body slime leading to infection in the fish following release.

The fish is still netted in the traditional manner but it can be handled inside the net and then released.

Jaw grips

These grips fasten securely to the lower jaw and allow the fish to be lifted from the water, unhooked and released. They are designed to be used on larger-sized fish.

When using grips, the fish are gripped by the lower jaw and then lifted by both the grips and placing the palm of the hand under the fish to support it. This avoids putting all of the fish's weight on its jaw when lifting.

Barbless hooks

Flattening the barb of the hook with pliers makes for the easy release of any fish. It is very popular when fishing with lures but can also be used with many forms of bait fishing.

The key here is to keep the line

did you know ...

SEASICKNESS

The first time you go to sea is always full of excitement and expectation. As you move out of the harbour or river into the open sea the boat will rise and fall with the movement of the ocean swell. At first the movement feels quite strange but you will get used to it quickly. For many first time anglers this movement can also cause seasickness.

Seasickness happens when the fluid in your middle ear (which maintains your balance) moves about in response to the motion of the boat. This movement eventually caused nausea and vomiting.

Being seasick is not a good way to start your seagoing career.

To avoid seasickness, get a good night's sleep before you go out, eat a simple breakfast of cereal, toast, tea or coffee and take an anti seasickness tablet before you leave home. Make sure you and your parents read the instruction so you take the correct dose as seasickness pills can cause some side effects.

tight once the fish is hooked, this holds the fish securely on the hook.

Often the fish can be released simply by easing line pressure at the side of the boat. Otherwise, it is netted and lifted aboard and the hook or lure can be easily removed.

The other advantage of barbless hooks is they can be easily and far less painfully removed if you are the one to get hooked!

CATCHING A BIG ONE

One of the great thrills of fishing is to catch your first big fish. How big it really is does not matter, at the time it will be important to you.

The problem is that at the time there will probably be lots of things happening, very few of which will be helpful to you. Often the first big fish will be purely accidental, you just find yourself connected to a big one and make the best of it.

You can improve the odds of catching a big fish if you live bait regularly, use lures or set baits deliberately for big fish. If you are going to try for large fish make sure

It's easy to get excited with your first big catch.

HINT BOX

Keeping fish alive

Live bait can be vital for capturing big fish and a tank of water is essential for keeping them available for use during the fishing session.

Many anglers also use their bait tanks or fish wells to store their captured fish and keep them alive. This is particularly important in modern tournaments where the fish are weighed in alive and then released.

Other anglers may keep a couple of fish alive until they catch a better one and then release the smaller fish. This means they only keep a couple of very good fish to eat and let the rest of them go.

Bait tanks or wet wells are often built into modern boats but it is also easy to fit a bait tank.

The tank needs to be big enough to hold the target fish and is fitted so it can't move around in a rocking boat.

An inlet pipe is fitted with an electronically powered submersible bait pump bringing water into the tank with an exhaust fitting allowing the used water to flow out through the hull or stern of the boat.

Once fitted, a tank will hold your bait and your fish in good shape until you use them or release them.

you use gear that can handle them, it makes the job much easier.

The first thing you need when you hook a big fish is control. Despite the excitement you need to stay steady so that you do things correctly and don't lose the fish through your own actions. Try to keep a clear mind and

remember exactly what happened during the fight so that you can correct it or improve on it next time.

If you are fishing with your parents or a friend who has caught good fish before, listen to their advice and try to follow their directions. If there are other people around who are suddenly offering you advice, yelling, or who want to 'help' just ignore them or if necessary tell them nicely to go away.

It is your fish, you hooked it and you can land it. Even if you lose it, it was still your fish and you will benefit from, the experience. Even the very best of anglers lose big fish now and again, it is a fact of life.

However, your job is to catch that fish, not worry about losing it. If the fish takes a lot of line let it run, do not increase the drag. Your drag should have been set correctly when you started fishing and it should still be all right. If your drag is too light, tighten it with quarter turns of the drag knob, don't take a full turn, it may be too much of an increase.

Keep good pressure on the fish, do not allow any slack line. This can usually be achieved by keeping the rod tip high in the air, not pointed down at the water. When the fish stops running, tire it by using the pump and wind technique. Don't be in a big hurry, it is much better to tire the fish while it is out away from you than to have a big, fresh fish, thrashing and lunging at close quarters. That is when fish are often lost.

When the fish allows, keep pumping it back to you. Big fish often make more than one run; though the other runs are not normally as far as the first. Again when it runs, don't try and stop it this will only snap the line. When the fish is close have your fishing buddy or whoever is fishing with you net the fish.

If you are fishing alone you may have to do it yourself, which is easy, you just need to tire the fish a little more.

The best combination is to work with a friend or family who fish together regularly. Teamwork and

did you know ...

HOW TO TELL THE AGE OF A FISH

The age of a fish is determined by two methods, reading the growth rings on the scales or by examining the ear stones or otoliths. In both cases ring patterns are laid down, which can accurately be followed to establish the age of a fish.

With scales, it is possible to see clearly defined patterns or rings called 'circuli' when the scale is viewed through a low powered microscope. They can also be seen but not easily counted by looking through a magnifying glass. In slow growing fish the rings are closer than in fast growing fish. In times of stress, particularly in winter when food is scarce, a definite change occurs to the structure of the scale. This is known as the 'winter band' and is used to calculate the age of the fish.

Using the ear stones or otoliths takes a bit of scientific know-how both to find the bones and have them cut into an histological cross section, which is stained to show the rings. However, once this process is complete very accurate ageing of the fish can be conducted.

Again, the ageing process is shown by rings but it is often very clearly laid down in the calcium carbonate structures of the ear stones.

Some fish like dolphin fish grow really fast, reaching 10 kilograms in less than a year. Other fish like nannygai grow very slowly averaging only one centimetre a year.

Knowing how fast a fish grows and when it reaches its breeding age is very important to scientists and for the management of the fishery.

mutual trust are important when landing big fish or just enjoying a day's fishing.

Just remember when that first big one comes along—stay calm and cool and enjoy the action. You'll remember it forever and it is one of life's great memories. And don't forget to take a photo either.

CHAPTER 9

CATCHING CRABS

Crabbing is a fun way to add something different to your catch.

It doesn't take much effort but you do need to watch your fingers as both blue swimmers and mud crabs can and will clamp their powerful claws on anyone who is unwary or careless when handling them. Blue swimmers really hurt but mud crabs can bite off or break a finger.

Crabs are part of the marine eco-system and turn up in all shapes and sizes. Most of the small species of crabs make good bait but are too small to eat. However, both blue swimmers and mud crabs grow to a large size and they are extremely good eating.

Crabs are basically scavengers, feeding on whatever they find but they are also capable hunters and can actually catch a wide range of fish.

Crabs will sometimes grab a baited fishing line and either get hooked or tangled. Usually, they just hang on like a heavy weight and the angler leads them to the boat or shore only to see them drop off the line as soon as they think they are in danger.

Crabs that grab a baited line can often be led to a waiting landing net once you know that it is indeed a crab. While you might miss it the first time, once you know how they feel on the end of the line you can usually tell when a crab has your bait.

The trick is to have someone submerge the landing net while you gently lead the crab towards it. When the crab is close enough to drop into the net, just lift the landing net firmly from below and the crab will be captured.

Catching a crab this way is a bit of a fluke, but you can target them quite specifically with traps and snares.

Witch's hats

The most common and cheapest method of catching crabs is with a snare known as a witch's hat. Witch's hats can be bought at most tackle stores.

This device is a ring of galvanised wire with a light mesh net around the edges. The mesh is pulled together at the top and a small float is added. This small float keeps the

net suspended and gives it the classic 'witch's hat' shape. There is a length of rope attached to the float to allow you to retrieve the snare or tie it off.

The one thing to check is that the rope is long enough for the depth of water where you want to fish. When you buy a witch's hat they only come with about three metres of rope attached, so you may need to add extra rope, particularly if fishing off a wharf or jetty.

There is a light rope across the frame and the bait is tied securely to the middle of the rope. The bait is usually a fish head or fish frame or some pilchards in a little plastic mesh purse.

You can use a witch's hat or several witches hats off any jetty. While you fish, the snares may catch you a crab or two.

The best results come from using a boat to set the snares on the deep edges of drop-offs, around the edges of weedbeds, in creek mouths and along channel edges. Always check the snares every hour or so as the crabs may become hopelessly entangled if you leave the snares down too long.

When setting the snares from a boat always make sure you have a float on the end of the rope with your name and address written on the float.

Crab dillies

Crab dillies are also made from a wire hoop, but rather than snare the crab they act as a cradle.

The dilly lies flat on the bottom allowing the crab easy access to the bait set in the middle of the hoop. When the angler lifts the dilly the crab's legs and swimmers fall through the mesh and water pressure keeps the crab in place, provided the angler pulls in rapidly.

did you know ...

LARGEST CRABS

Crabs range from tiny microscopic zooplankton through to huge beasts weighing up to 15 kilograms.

The king crab found in deep water off Australia's southern and Tasmanian coasts is amongst the largest with a shell size of ove 40 cm and weight of up to 14 kg. These massive crabs are caught in traps in water about 200 metres deep and are a prized and highly valuable catch.

Larger and even more valuable, the giant spider crabs caught off the coast of Japan is weird looking and is the largest crab. As it's name suggests, it looks like a giant spider, with a leg span of up to two metres and a weight of 15 kilograms. A strange looking animal indeed.

Getting the witch's hat ready to drop.

Crab trap

Crab traps come in a variety of shapes and designs. Essentially they provide an enclosed space, which is baited with fish heads, fish frames or whole fish. Cone shaped openings allow entry to the crabs but at the same time makes it difficult for them to escape. The trap is set in a selected area and can be left for long periods as the crabs tend not to leave the trap.

Traps are good for holiday fishing as they can be set and left overnight. Many crab traps are designed to flatten out for easy storage and transport. These are the best choice if you need to carry them in the car or on public transport.

Always set crab traps with the entry nozzles facing parallel to the current as the crabs will move up the current following the smell of the bait through the water.

Rules

Catching crabs is covered by different rules in each state and it is important to check what regulations apply in your area. Your local fishing tackle shop or fisheries officer can give you the right advice.

Fact Box

DANGER ALERT

HOW TO HANDLE A CRAB

WARNING: *Handling crabs can be dangerous. Take extreme care.*

When you catch a blue swimmer or mud crab the real trick is to handle it properly and never get caught by the crab's nippers. Crabs are strong, fast movers and have a very bad attitude when captured.

The only place to safely hold a crab is to use your thumb and forefinger, grasping both back legs (flippers), right up against the body or shell of the crab.

Crabs have extremely good eyesight and a free moving, unrestrained crab can be very difficult to handle. The best way to position a crab is to use a shoed foot coming from behind to firmly pin the rear half of the crab, then grasping it as described.

Any crab considered too hard to handle can be subdued by placing it, and if necessary the trap, in a cool room or freezer. The crab will soon become slow moving and easier to handle. Covering it in ice will have the same result.

Mud crabs caught in traps should be emptied from the trap into a bucket without touching the crab. Have only one crab per bucket or they will damage each other.

CHAPTER 10

CLEANING FISH

Fish are really healthy food, so it's important to look after your catch and make sure it doesn't spoil.

The best way to keep your catch from spoiling is to have an esky with some ice in it. This may not always be possible but there are other options.

You can use a keeper net, which is suspended in the water and will keep most of the fish alive until you are finished fishing. A wet sugar bag is also satisfactory, as is a bucket of seawater.

The vital thing is to make sure the fish are not left out in the sun or they will spoil. Fish spoil faster in warmer weather so if the day is hot and you catch some good fish it will be important to get them cleaned and on ice or in a refrigerator fairly quickly.

The other key is to only keep the fish you want to eat. Keep a good fish or two for food and release the rest. This makes the cleaning job easy.

Cleaning the Catch

In order to enjoy your fish as food they need to be cleaned. There are two basic ways of doing this. One is to remove the scales and gut and cook the fish whole. The other is to remove the fleshy, edible sides of the fish, known as filleting.

The way you clean your catch depends on lots of factors. These include the size of the fish, the type of fish and how you or someone else wants to cook it.

The start of the cleaning process usually involves scaling the fish. You do this by using a scaler or the back of a knife. Hold the fish down firmly with one hand and work the knife or scaler from the tail towards the head, removing the scales as you go. When you finish one side turn the fish over and complete the job.

To clean fish properly you need a sharp knife. Sharp knives need respect—they can bite careless fingers. Always use the knife so that you are cutting away from your hands and body. This applies whether you are cutting bait or cleaning fish.

Gutting fish
The simplest way to clean any fish is to gut it. You can leave the head on or you can remove it, it depends on you. Leaving the head on adds to its appearance on the table, and you might be surprised to learn there is a lot of edible meat on the head of a fish.

To gut a fish, turn the fish on its side with its head facing away from you. Use one hand to hold the fish securely in place. Insert the point of the knife into the anal vent and cut along the abdomen of the fish until you reach the area where the head joins the body, encasing the gills.

At this point cut horizontally across the neck just linking the cut you made along the stomach.

Use your index finger and thumb to open up the fish from the gills downwards. Remove the gills and all the gut. Gently use the blade of the knife to remove any material left in the stomach cavity.

When you've removed all the gut and gills, wash the fish thoroughly, and store it either in the refrigerator or freezer.

Filleting fish

To fillet a fish you need to make a cut just behind the head and then cut down the spine of the fish. Angle the blade of the knife towards the tail and then slice along the back of the fish staying as close to the spine as possible.

A good fillet will remove almost all of the meat from a fish. The head and remaining frame is then disposed of or kept frozen for later use as crab bait.

FISH FACT

PUFFER FISH

The puffer fish can blow itself up like a balloon. When it is removed from the water it quickly gulps downs large amounts of air and water till it is about three times its original size. When you throw it back it floats around upside down until it can expel the air and water from its body.

Puffer fish are poisonous to eat and contain a deadly toxin called Tetrodotoxin, the same toxin found in the blue ringed octopus. Yet, despite this fact they are a prized eating fish in Japan where they are known as 'fugu'. However they are only prepared by Japanese chefs who have graduated from a fugu-cooking school and who know how to remove the poison from the fish.

Cleaning fish as soon as possible after catching it keeps it fresh and tasting its best.

When you finish cleaning the fish, wash down your working area, don't leave any bits and pieces lying around, wash your knife and finally make sure you give your hands a good clean too.

Stomach contents

When cleaning fish it is often worth checking what your catch has been eating. Sometimes it can provide a real clue to help increase your catch.

As an example, the fish in the photograph here is a tailor normally considered a surface fish yet it was full of little flathead, which are definitely bottom fish. The fish was caught when a small tangle meant the lure fell to the bottom and the fish struck as the lure was wound off the bottom. Once that first fish was caught, the angler kept letting the lure sink to the bottom and then retrieving it. He kept catching the tailor. Obviously the tailor were feeding on the bottom and the flathead were a great clue.

The same can happen with any fish. If the fish are full of whitebait you should use whitebait or a lure that looks like a whitebait.

Trout anglers use stomach contents regularly. If the trout are full of black beetles then black flies or black lures may yield extra strikes. Checking stomach contents will increase your knowledge of what your fish eat.

Fact Box

KNIVES

An important part of any anglers equipment, a fishing knife is worth spending a little extra on in order to buy a good quality stainless steel blade that resists rust. Every angler needs a knife to clean the catch and prepare the bait.

There are many types of fishing knives: short, sturdy knives for slicing tough natural bait such as cunjevoi, the all purpose knife for bait preparation and fish cleaning, long-bladed filleting knives and others.

The important thing with knives is to buy one that suits your fishing. For most anglers this means a combination fillet knife with a scaler on the back. You can also buy a scaler very cheaply so don't worry if the knife you want does not have a scaler as part of the blade.

You need to keep the knife sharp too, so buy a fine grained sharpening stone to help keep your knife properly sharpened and easy to use.

CHAPTER 11

DANGEROUS FISH

Fishing is supposed to be full of fun, but all anglers should be aware that there are a few fish that can inflict painful wounds or even more painful stings.

Most anglers learn quickly about what can bite or sting and take appropriate action but for the beginner it is not always easy and a few points should be noted.

Bites

Many species of fish have savage teeth and it is obvious that if you put your fingers in there trying to retrieve the hook, you will receive a vicious wound.

There is a natural respect for fish with big teeth but people, mainly beginners, still manage to get bitten. Even experienced anglers like the authors have been bitten—so don't get careless.

Other fish with less obvious cutting teeth, but powerful jaws like bream and snapper can still crush a careless small finger just as they can crush a shellfish.

The answer is to respect all fish until you know how to handle them. Fish with obvious sharp teeth may need pliers, fish with crushing teeth may need more care.

In all cases where risk is involved, cut your hook off and tie on another. It is so simple and if you keep the fish you'll get your hook back when you clean the fish.

Spines and spikes

Some fish have very sharp spines, spikes and gill covers. These may not be poisonous but they can still inflict a nasty injury.

Flathead in particular have a very dangerous spine at the side of their head, right at the end of their gill cover. This spike can inflict a bad cut if the fish is not handled with care. Of all the common, non-poisonous estuary fish around, flathead are the hardest to handle. If you are going to keep them, it is often just as easy to drop them in the esky or other storage space and, once secure, cut the hook off and tie on another. Using a pair of fish tongs is also useful when handling flathead. With small flathead destined for release, handle them with extreme care in a wet towel, they can still hurt.

Lots of other fish like bream and snapper have spikes as part of their defence mechanisms. These fish can be handled easily with a grip that has the breastbone of the fish in the palm of your hand and your thumb and fingers located firmly down each side of the fish near the gill covers.

While a few small spikes and scratches will happen in handling fish, a little practice and confidence will soon teach you how to do it with a minimum of hassles.

Fish that sting

Some fish have a powerful toxin loaded into their spines. Many of these fish are well known, with the stingray and catfish being most commonly identified, but there are several more that all anglers should be familiar with. If you do get stung, treat the wound with warm water and seek medical advice from a doctor or local hospital.

The following list of fish need plenty of respect and should not be handled.

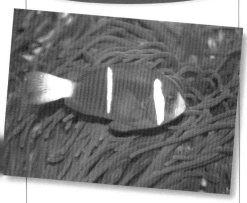

FISH FACT

ANEMONE FISH

Sea anemones have very powerful stinging cells built into their tentacles. Any small fish or shrimp that wanders into an anemone will set off these stinging cells, paralysing them, and allowing the anemone to move it slowly down to its mouth. The paralysed prey is then slowly eaten alive.

One fish, the anemone fish, has adapted to live its entire life within the stinging tentacles. Each different type of anemone has different species of anemone fish adapted to live with it. The anemone fish fools the host into not stinging it by using the same chemical mix in its protective body covering as the anemone. The advantage for the anemone fish is that so long as it stays with its stinging host not much is likely to attack or eat it.

A smart idea and one of nature's great adaptations.

The movie character Nemo by the way was a species of anemone fish known as a clownfish and there are about 30 different species worldwide.

Stingray

The name says it all. Most of the ray family carry a poisonous barb along their tail. This can be driven very accurately by the ray at anything it sees as a threat. If you catch a stingray do not handle it at all, just cut the line below the swivel and let it go.

When wading on sandbanks it also pays to shuffle along rather than take big steps, as it is possible to stand on a stingray.

Catfish

The best advice is to handle this fish just like a stingray—cut it off. Making a mistake while trying to get the hook back can be very painful.

Freshwater catfish can cause quite a sting too but they are not as painful as the saltwater variety. Freshwater catfish are a good table fish but like all catfish they have three barbed spines just behind the head. One spine is on top and one spine is on either side of the body.

Scorpion fish

Fortescue, bullrout, red rock cod and scorpion fish are members of the scorpion fish family and the 13 dorsal spines on top of the fish can deliver a ferocious sting. These fish can come in all sizes but their basic shape remains the same.

The easiest way to handle these fish is to use pliers to remove the hook and just drop the fish back in the water. You can use pliers to hold the fish and get the hook out by hand if you wish.

Scorpion fish like this red rock cod have a fiery toxin in their spines handle them with great care.

It is vital that you avoid those spines at the top of the fish's back.

Happy moments or black trevally

These are a common temperate and warm water species, again with toxic dorsal spines. These fish are a caught regularly from jetties and in estuaries.

All the spines on these fish are poisonous so the fish should be handled with care. Avoid handling these fish, use fish grips or fish tongs instead.

Poisonous fish

Some fish are poisonous to eat. The main ones are toadfish, cowfish and boxfish. They don't feel or even look like they would be good to eat and if you do eat them they could kill you. So don't take these fish home, just throw them back in the water.

ABOVE: All members of the catfish family have poisonous spikes located on the top and on the sides just behind their head.

BELOW: Spinefoots, happy moments or black trevally it doesn't matter what their name really is their spines can sting you severely.

CHAPTER 12
WEATHER

The state of the weather can have a big effect on your catches and your personal comfort.

Because most of us go fishing for fun, the best days are always those with light winds and calm water. This relates to personal comfort and enjoyment of the day just as much as it relates to catches of fish. However, fish live in a very different world below the water. There is no rain or wind blowing under the surface. Yet the fish still seem to be affected by the weather.

The reasons for this are not well known but bad weather, particularly strong winds, usually means bad fishing. Days with heavy cloud cover and perhaps a little rain but with no wind are often very good days to go fishing. The reason relates to the lack of light available to the fish. In the dull light they can't see the trap of a baited hook as well as on a bright day.

Other things that can influence the fish include a rapidly falling barometer, which will usually put fish off the bite.

Bright, calm days with clear water will also make the fish very wary. They are worried about predators and very cautious about biting in such conditions.

Strong winds make most types of fishing difficult. The only advantage may be longer casts if the wind is blowing from behind you. The problem with strong wind is that it disrupts your usual fishing style. It's hard to set your gear comfortably and often the fish just don't bite very well on windy days.

Weather is an important part of your day's fishing so always take note of the forecast for the day and remember to keep in a diary the weather conditions when you do catch fish. You can use this information to repeat these catches.

Time and tide

Fish can be caught at any time of the day but they bite best early in the morning and late in the afternoon.

This is because these times allow the fish better feeding opportunities with low light levels, which help protect them from predators.

However, some fish are available at most times throughout the day and a little experience and careful watching of other anglers will soon tell you what is around and when.

If fishing in saltwater you should always be aware of what the tide is doing, it will have an important bearing on your fishing. Even simple things like which side of the wharf you fish on will be determined by the movement of the tide. You always fish on the side of the boat or wharf that has the current carrying your line away from you. Fishing the other way your line would be carried under the boat or wharf, which would make fishing very difficult.

Tidal movements have a very strong influence on the feeding habits of many fish.

A rising tide for instance, allows

fish access to feeding areas like sand flats, weedbeds and mangroves and a falling tide forces them back into the channels. Predatory fish that feed on smaller fish are more likely to be active on a falling tide as the small fish, shrimps and crabs are forced back into the channels by the tide. The time of still water between tides is always a prime feeding time for most fish. The lack of tide allows them easy movement to search for food.

Tidal forces affect each area differently as well. Tides tend not to have very much effect in a big harbour, bay or lake, but they have a great influence in coastal rivers and the channels that feed lakes and bays.

The important thing is to know what the tide is doing during your fishing day. If you get results when the tide is at a particular point remember it and try to match that tide the next time you fish in the same place.

Personal protection

Fishermen need protection from the weather and the elements. All anglers need SPF 30+ sun protection whenever they go out. Sunburn is bad

---

Fact Box

BAROMETERS

A barometer is an instrument for measuring atmospheric pressure, which is the basis of accurate weather forecasting. 1016 hectopascals is normal air pressure. A number lower than this is low pressure and higher is high pressure.

Many species of fish are responsive to changes in atmospheric pressure. For instance, pelagic game fish and sharks usually feed actively and strike well immediately before a spell of bad weather and high wind. Similarly, when the atmospheric pressure begins to fall, mulloway may come on the bite.

Trout are much affected by atmospheric pressure, when the barometer begins to rise, so do the trout.

Many native freshwater fish are very dependant on air pressure. Cod, bass and golden perch bite best when the barometer is high and rising.

Our local snapper fishermen always say 'when the air pressure is ten twenty (1020) you'll catch plenty.'

---

news, so sun safe clothing like long sleeve cotton shirts and a hat is also a good idea.

The wind and spray can also make you very cold so a spray jacket is a handy thing to carry. They weigh next-to nothing and can fit into a very small space in your bag, so pack a spray jacket.

Always remember to dress for the expected weather conditions. If it is going to be cold then take the necessary clothes, you can always take them off if it gets hot.

A rolling storm front heads across an estuary. These fronts often have dangerous winds and heavy rain.

CHAPTER 13

ETHICS & THE ENVIRONMENT

Catching fish is a very natural pastime, practised by people since the beginning of time. The aim of going fishing is to have fun and to catch fish that are good to eat.

Everyone who goes fishing has a duty to care for the environment. Without clean water and a healthy environment we will have no fish. As an angler you are using a natural resource and you have a responsibility both to the fish and the environment. It is important to keep only the fish you want for food and bait. All unwanted fish should be returned to the water without injury.

Some fish like eels, stingrays and saltwater catfish are considered as vermin. Anglers sometimes kill these unwanted fish so they can remove their fish hooks. These fish though have an important role to play in the marine eco-system and you can get injured trying to handle them anyway. The simple answer is to just cut the line near the fish and release it—hooks are cheap.

There will also be plenty of small, unwanted species and undersized fish in your captures. Again you should respect these fish and let them go.

HINT BOX

Angling etiquette

A good attitude and civil manners are necessary if you and everyone else are going to enjoy fishing.

We go fishing for fun, relaxation, adventure and to learn about the natural world not for agro or bad behaviour. At times we may be fishing close to others and this means respecting the people and the water space they are using. The same applies when in a boat. Always give people in other boats enough room to fish, particularly if they are there first.

If the fish are coming from a certain area always ask if they mind if you get close. A pleasant attitude and please and thank you put everyone at ease and keeps the fun in the fishing.

Always remember you are out to have a good time and so is everyone else. Treat people well and you will usually get the same in return. If you do strike people with a bad attitude just move away, don't let their problems ruin your day.

Keep within the rules

Fishing rules vary quite markedly from state to state and it is important for all anglers to know what is right and what is wrong when they go fishing. Your local Fisheries office and most tackle stores will have copies of these rules.

The important things to learn are the legal size of fish you can keep, the bag limits that apply to the fish you keep and any protected species so that you can put them back carefully. You also need to know any closed seasons or restrictions that might apply to your fishing area.

Keeping within the rules is vitally important as it protects our fish resources and provides a framework for ethical angling.

It is important to know the rules, make sure you do.

If you use the aquatic environment you also have a responsibility to care for it. Don't throw any litter into the water. If you buy bait in plastic packets, make sure you either take the packets home for disposal or put them in the nearest litter bin.

If you want to be a real angler you need to care for the fish and the water they live in.

did you know ...

FISH NEED OXYGEN

Oxygen is the gas our lungs extract from the air we breath it is what keeps us and all other animals alive. While mammals extract their vital oxygen through their lungs, fish extract oxygen from the water using their gills. Dissolved oxygen is present in water and it is just as essential to fish as it is to mammals. Dissolved oxygen levels in water are governed by a range of factors including water movement, salinity and temperature.

Algae and aquatic plants also turn carbon dioxide into oxygen through photosynthesis during daylight hours, just as land plants do and this oxygen is also released into the water. Some areas always have high oxygen levels in the water. Surf zones, below waterfalls and fast running water always hold more oxygen than still water. Cold water is always better oxygenated than warm water, and running water better oxygenated than still.

Different fish need different levels of oxygen with fast swimming species like tuna and kingfish needing more oxygen than slow moving species such as flounder and flathead.

ABOVE: Colder water where mixing ensures high oxygen content can produce more fish with the urge to feed.

LEFT: A healthy environment provides for a wide range of birds, animals and fish. It is your job to keep it that way.

CHAPTER 14

SAFETY

General fishing may not be in the same class of danger and injury as contact sports like football, karate or boxing, fishing still has its share of cuts, bumps and bruises.

Every year you hear of fishermen who have fallen from boats or been washed off of rocky ledges to their deaths. Taking a reasonable amount of care can virtually eliminate the chance of serious injury but unfortunately you will probably hurt yourself when fishing at some time in your fishing life—it is impossible to avoid all accidents. Luckily, the majority of these are minor. As most of us learn by our mistakes we tend not to repeat things that hurt us once. With experience you will have fewer accidents, here we are attempting to prevent or to reduce the effect of accidents.

It always helps if you learn some of your fishing skills from someone who knows what they are doing. They will also show you the dangers. However, in the end you are responsible for yourself.

Anywhere around water can be dangerous. Jetties, especially ones that are used by commercial or recreational boaters, have many

obstructions and potential tripping hazards. The pylons are often covered by shellfish that can inflict nasty cuts. Falling or being thrown from a boat is a constant possibility. Inland, the banks and edges of lakes and rivers are often steep and undercut, while the apparently firm bed of a lake or river is often soft mud covering deep holes. The temperature of the water, especially in the southern States and inland below dam walls where water is released from the bottom of a lake, is often very cold and can seriously affect the ability to swim of someone who finds themselves suddenly immersed in it.

Recently laws have been passed in several Australian States that make the wearing of life jackets—known as personal flotation devices or PFDs—compulsory when in small boat and / or when the boat is moving. Check your State's requirements as to whether you are required to wear a PFD, but we recommend that you wear one at all times when in

a boat regardless of the law. If you are using an inflatable PFD ensure that you know how to inflate it in an emergency.

Finally, you cannot control the actions of other anglers around you. Be aware of what they are doing and whether it poses any risk to you. If necessary move away from them—your safety is more important than any fishing spot.

Here are some hints to help you have a safe and happy fishing trip:
- Always fish with a friend or two. This is especially important when fishing in remote areas where you can become lost and in areas where the water is active like from the rocks, the beach or from a boat.
- Take care around obvious hazards like rocks, oysters, cliffs, slippery or undercut river and lake banks and boat ramps.
- Take care when fishing around areas what have a lot of activity, like jetties or boat ramps, and at the start and end of a fishing trip when you may be excited or tired.
- Learn and follow the safety rules when in a boat or canoe.
- Keep the area within a boat clear to avoid tripping or falling.
- Learn where the safety equipment in a boat is kept and how to use it.
- Knives and hooks are sharp. Learn to use them safely and store them where they can't hurt anyone when they are not in use.
- Learn how to recognise and handle dangerous fish. Remember that most fish are dangerous if handled incorrectly.
- Never take risks with things you don't know or understand.
- Be prepared to ask for help from people who do know what they are doing. Most anglers are friendly and are ready to help someone who is willing to learn.
- Take your time, many accidents happen because people rush when a more steady, deliberate approach is needed.
- If you are fishing with an experienced angler or boater do what they tell you. With their experience they will know how to avoid problems.

Use your eyes and brain and keep your awareness of personal safety high.